ROYAL BOTANIC GARDENS KEW

A Souvenir Guide

Contents

Introduction

About Kew Gardens

The Royal Botanic Gardens, Kew cover an area of over 121 hectares (300 acres) on the south bank of the Thames in south-west London. The vast number and variety of plants means the nature of Kew Gardens changes with the seasons. Out in the grounds, and inside the plant houses, thousands of specimens progress through their annual cycles, flowering, fruiting, growing, resting. All year long, there are plants to be seen at their glorious best.

But Kew is much more than one of the world's finest showpiece gardens. It's an internationally respected centre of scientific excellence, identifying and classifying plants, researching their structure, chemistry and genetics; collecting and conserving endangered species; maintaining reference collections and sharing all this knowledge with interested parties throughout the world.

About this book

This Souvenir Guide tells you what there is to see, where it is, and how to get there.

On the next page, the map, 'Finding your way around Kew', has basic information about the Gardens, the public facilities, the main plant houses and plantings. To help you on your way, there are orientation diagrams from each gate.

Kew is a very seasonal pleasure, so there are four seasonal maps, telling you when which plants are at their best. After each map, you will find directions for pleasant seasonal walks, one short, one longer, with what to look out for and the approximate time each takes at a leisurely pace.

There are separate sections for the major buildings and garden areas. Each starts with key features, then gives more detailed information, combining a little history with a lot of interesting facts.

Finally, you can read about Kew's past development and its role today - more important now than ever in its lifetime of more than 200 years.

GENERAL INFORMATION

The Gardens open at 9.30 am every day of the year except Christmas Day and New Year's Day. They close at times between 4 pm during the winter and 6.30 pm (7.30 pm on weekends and public holidays) throughout the summer. The glasshouses and galleries close earlier than the Gardens, so it is worth visiting them first of all. The Information Line (020 8332 5655) gives current information and the Kew Gardens website is packed with information:- www.kew.org

KEW EXPLORER

See more of Kew with the Kew Explorer, an eco-friendly, gas-powered 72-seat people mover which plies a circular route around the Gardens, starting and finishing at the Victoria Gate Centre. It's a hop on, hop off service for ticket holders, with stops close by the main buildings and other places of interest around Kew. You can buy your ticket at the Gates, the Shops or from the driver. There is space for one person in a wheelchair and there's also room for folded wheelchairs and pushchairs. Please call 020 8332 5615/5617 for current costs, and timings and route.

GOOD GARDENS FOOD

You will find a wide choice of food in the Gardens, ranging from hot meals with wine to snacks, sandwiches and ice creams. And, of course, there's always somewhere for a reviving cup of tea or coffee. It depends on the time of year which venues are open: your free visitor map will give current details when you visit. Alternatively, you are welcome to bring your own picnic to the Gardens.

SHOPS

There is a wide range of books, postcards and exclusive Kew gifts and souvenirs including stationery, scarves, chinaware and prints in the Victoria Gate Centre and White Peaks. All profits from the Shops go to support Kew's vital scientific work.

SPECIAL NEEDS INFORMATION

The Gardens are accessible to wheelchairs, except for the Marine Display in the Palm House. Wheelchairs may be borrowed, but please book in advance to be sure (020 8332 5121). Please ask about the 'Discovery' service - a bus tour of the Gardens carefully designed for people with special needs. This needs to be booked in advance.

SAFETY & FIRST AID

There are water features in the Gardens and visitors with small children are asked to be especially watchful for their safety. For First Aid or other help, see the staff at the ticket offices or one of the Constables - they are in police uniforms. But you will find all Kew Gardens staff are very willing to help, so if you need a hand, just ask.

PLEASE REMEMBER

Kew's plants are valuable specimens and visitors are requested not to touch them and not to climb the trees. Similarly, bicycles, trikes, scooters and skates; ball games or any sporting activities are not allowed. However, unlike many gardens, you are welcome to walk on the grass! To preserve the peace and tranquillity of the Gardens, so much enjoyed by visitors, the use of radios and cassette players is not permitted. No animals are allowed, except for guide dogs. Still and video cameras may be used for personal enjoyment, but for commercial use, please contact the Press Office (020 8332 5607).

The information given here and throughout this Souvenir Guide is current at the time of going to press. As a result of new developments, plantings in the Gardens may change without notice. Please consult the visitor map, provided free of charge at the gates, for more information and details of any seasonal changes.

When planning a visit it is wise to call the Information Line (020 8332 5655) for the latest details about the Gardens.

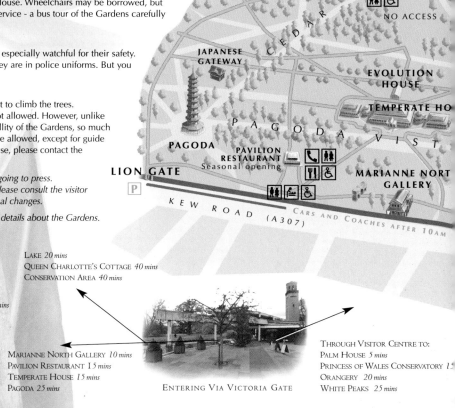

JAPANESE GATEWAY *10 mins*
QUEEN CHARLOTTE'S COTTAGE *20 mins*
CONSERVATION AREA *20 mins*

PAGODA *5 mins*

PAVILION RESTAURANT *10 mins*
TEMPERATE HOUSE *15 mins*
MARIANNE NORTH GALLERY *15 mins*

LAKE *20 mins*
QUEEN CHARLOTTE'S COTTAGE *40 mins*
CONSERVATION AREA *40 mins*

MARIANNE NORTH GALLERY *10 mins*
PAVILION RESTAURANT *15 mins*
TEMPERATE HOUSE *15 mins*
PAGODA *25 mins*

THROUGH VISITOR CENTRE TO:
PALM HOUSE *5 mins*
PRINCESS OF WALES CONSERVATORY *15*
ORANGERY *20 mins*
WHITE PEAKS *25 mins*

ENTERING VIA LION GATE

ENTERING VIA VICTORIA GATE

Finding your way around Kew

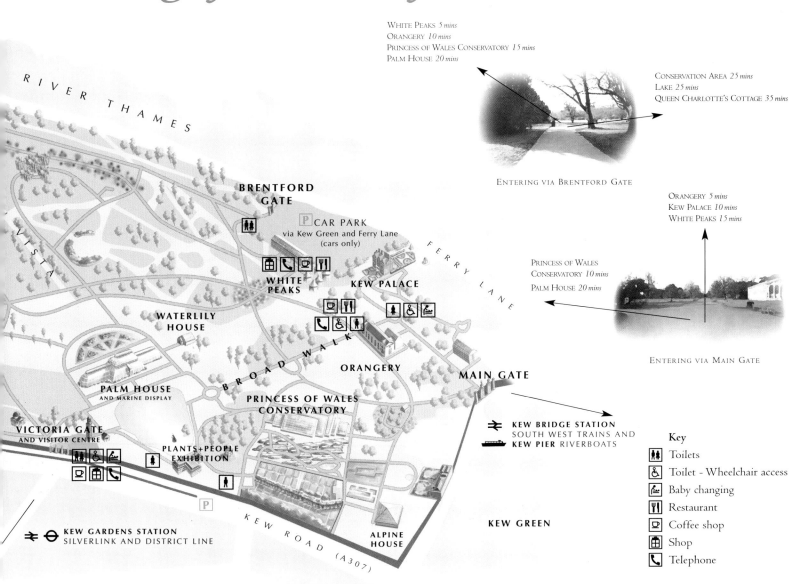

WHITE PEAKS 5 *mins*
ORANGERY 10 *mins*
PRINCESS OF WALES CONSERVATORY 15 *mins*
PALM HOUSE 20 *mins*

CONSERVATION AREA 25 *mins*
LAKE 25 *mins*
QUEEN CHARLOTTE'S COTTAGE 35 *mins*

ENTERING VIA BRENTFORD GATE

ORANGERY 5 *mins*
KEW PALACE 10 *mins*
WHITE PEAKS 15 *mins*

PRINCESS OF WALES
CONSERVATORY 10 *mins*
PALM HOUSE 20 *mins*

ENTERING VIA MAIN GATE

RIVER THAMES

VISTA

BRENTFORD GATE

P CAR PARK
via Kew Green and Ferry Lane
(cars only)

FERRY LANE

WHITE PEAKS

KEW PALACE

WATERLILY HOUSE

BROAD WALK

PALM HOUSE
AND MARINE DISPLAY

ORANGERY

MAIN GATE

VICTORIA GATE
AND VISITOR CENTRE

PLANTS+PEOPLE
EXHIBITION

PRINCESS OF WALES
CONSERVATORY

KEW BRIDGE STATION
SOUTH WEST TRAINS AND
KEW PIER RIVERBOATS

P

KEW GARDENS STATION
SILVERLINK AND DISTRICT LINE

KEW ROAD (A307)

ALPINE HOUSE

KEW GREEN

Key

	Toilets
	Toilet - Wheelchair access
	Baby changing
	Restaurant
	Coffee shop
	Shop
	Telephone

5

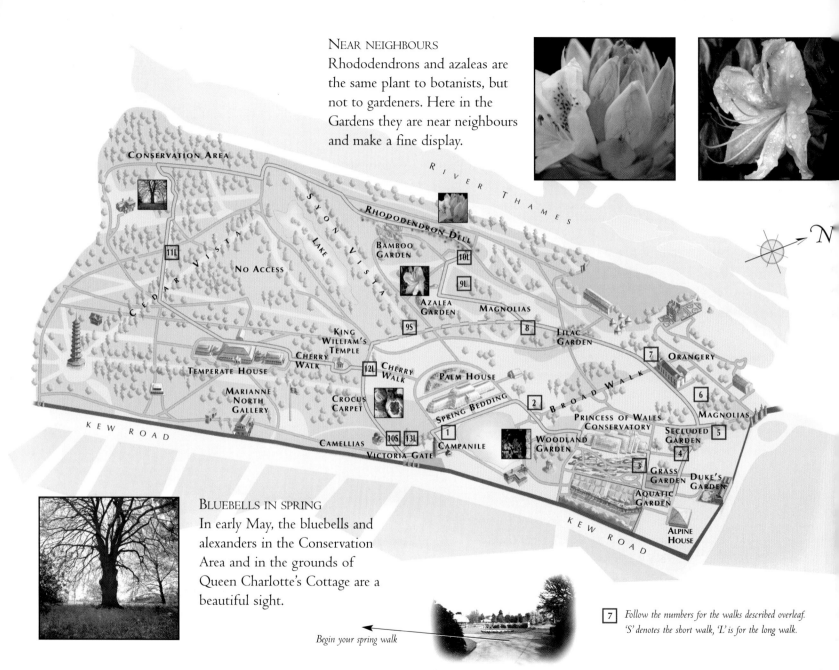

NEAR NEIGHBOURS
Rhododendrons and azaleas are the same plant to botanists, but not to gardeners. Here in the Gardens they are near neighbours and make a fine display.

CONSERVATION AREA

RIVER THAMES

SYON VISTA

LAKE

CEDAR VISTA

RHODODENDRON DELL

NO ACCESS

11L

BAMBOO GARDEN

10L

9L

AZALEA GARDEN

MAGNOLIAS

9S

8

LILAC GARDEN

KING WILLIAM'S TEMPLE

7

ORANGERY

CHERRY WALK

TEMPERATE HOUSE

12L

CHERRY WALK

PALM HOUSE

BROAD WALK

6

MARIANNE NORTH GALLERY

CROCUS CARPET

SPRING BEDDING

2

PRINCESS OF WALES CONSERVATORY

MAGNOLIAS

SECLUDED GARDEN

5

KEW ROAD

CAMELLIAS

10S 13L

1

CAMPANILE

WOODLAND GARDEN

4

VICTORIA GATE

3

GRASS GARDEN

DUKE'S GARDEN

AQUATIC GARDEN

ALPINE HOUSE

KEW ROAD

BLUEBELLS IN SPRING
In early May, the bluebells and alexanders in the Conservation Area and in the grounds of Queen Charlotte's Cottage are a beautiful sight.

Begin your spring walk

LEAVING THE VICTORIA GATE CENTRE

7 Follow the numbers for the walks described overleaf. 'S' denotes the short walk, 'L' is for the long walk.

6

Spring at Kew

Seasons and flowering times, especially in spring, can vary by up to three weeks so the periods below are only approximate. For up-to-date details of flowering, please call 020 8332 5655 or visit the website at www.kew.org

March to May sees the full spread of spring from fresh awakenings to bravura displays. There are crocuses en masse between the Victoria Gate Centre and King William's Temple and camellias on the way to the Marianne North Gallery. Daffodils and narcissi are naturalised all over the Gardens and the recent planting of daffodils either side of the Broad Walk are a fine sight.

The Cherry Walk can be stunning, as is the spring bedding outside the Palm House. Crab apple trees are in flower along with magnolias and wisterias.

You can see where the main flowering displays are on this map, and if you would like to try a favourite spring walk, see the next page.

OVER A MILLION AND A HALF CROCUSES
Reader's Digest sponsored the carpet of 1.6 million crocuses between King William's Temple and the Victoria Gate Centre on its 50th anniversary in 1987. In early 2001, they funded a three-year rejuvenation programme involving the planting of 700,000 new corms.

BABES IN THE WOOD
The Woodland Garden comes fully to life and here, as all over the Gardens, birds build their nests and, later on, feed their hungry broods.

Spring Walks

You can take a long or a short version of this walk. At a gentle pace, looking at plants, but not lingering, the short walk takes about one and a half to two hours, the long walk about an hour longer, starting and ending at the Victoria Gate Centre. You can follow the walk, which is on both paths and grass, from the description below and/or from the spring map on the previous page.

Bluebell

Magnolia

Camellia

1 Leaving the Visitor Centre, go past the Campanile and immediately turn left towards the Palm House. Turn right to walk the length of the Palm House, with the spring bedding displays on your left. There may be some waterfowl displaying on the Pond at mating time.

2 Turn right, away from the Palm House, go straight on at the roundabout and the Woodland Garden is ahead, bursting into life. Follow the path left and go through the Princess of Wales Conservatory to the north end, where there's an attractive seasonal display.

3 Turn right at the exit and take the second path left, past the pools of the Aquatic Garden and head right to the Alpine House with its collection of exquisite miniature spring flowers.

4 As you come out of the Alpine House, turn right and go up the path, past the Grass Garden (left) and Duke's Garden (right) to a huge stone pine tree, where there's a sign into the Secluded Garden. Go through and out the other side where, a little to the left, there's a wonderful display of wisteria on an old pergola.

5 Turn back from the pergola, past the Secluded Garden towards the Main Gate. Just past the path to the Orangery, there's a planting of magnolias which shouldn't be missed.

6 Go to the Orangery - maybe stopping there for a little light refreshment. Look down the Broad Walk with, in March and April, a mass of daffodils on either side - Wordsworth's 'golden host' is a perfect description.

short walk

long walk

7 With the Broad Walk on your left, head up the main path to an intersection by the pretty Lilac Garden, at its best in May. Now take the path forking left away from Brentford Gate and stroll along past a magnificent display of magnolias on your right.

8 Short walk or long walk?
Now you make your decision. For the short walk (around 15 minutes back to the Victoria Gate Centre), continue along the path past the magnolias. For the long walk (an extra hour, maybe more), turn right across the grass, following the Azalea Garden signs. The azaleas are an eye-opener in April and May.

Short walk:
9S Continue straight on after the magnolias, crossing one path and arriving at where five paths meet. Follow the sign to Victoria Gate and a few paces along there is a crossroads. On either side of you is the splendid Cherry Walk, with King William's Temple and the Temperate House to the right and the Palm House to the

left. Cross straight over towards the Temple of Bellona, and you will find thousands upon thousands of crocuses in early spring.

10S At the path by the Kew Road wall, look right at the camellias all along the path to the Marianne North Gallery - a unique collection of flower paintings well worth a visit. Otherwise, turn left and you will arrive back at the Victoria Gate Centre.

Long walk:
9L Walk over the grass into the Azalea Garden. After reaching the circle of beds turn right to join the path heading down towards the river, the Bamboo Garden and Rhododendron Dell.

10L Take one of three paths to the left, Bamboo Garden, Rhododendron Dell (as shown on the map) or turn left at the T-junction. Keep walking (they all meet up) past Syon Vista to the end of the path where you have to turn left. Turn immediately right towards Queen Charlotte's Cottage.

In the woods, turn left (singpost toilets) and walk past the lively bird feeding station until a fence shows the end of the Conservation Area.

11L Leave the path with a quick right and left turn and walk down the grass through the firs, crossing Cedar Vista and forking left towards the Temperate House where the crab apple trees are in flower. Either detour through the house, or continue round the outside, but head left towards King William's Temple along the mass of blossom in Cherry Walk.

12L At the crossroads after the temple, turn right (signpost Victoria Gate) and pass the Temple of Bellona, with thousands of crocuses all around.

13L Carry on down this path and, as you reach the T-junction by the Kew Road wall, look right at the camellias on the way to the Marianne North Gallery with its superb collection of flower paintings. Go and admire them, or turn left back to the Victoria Gate Centre.

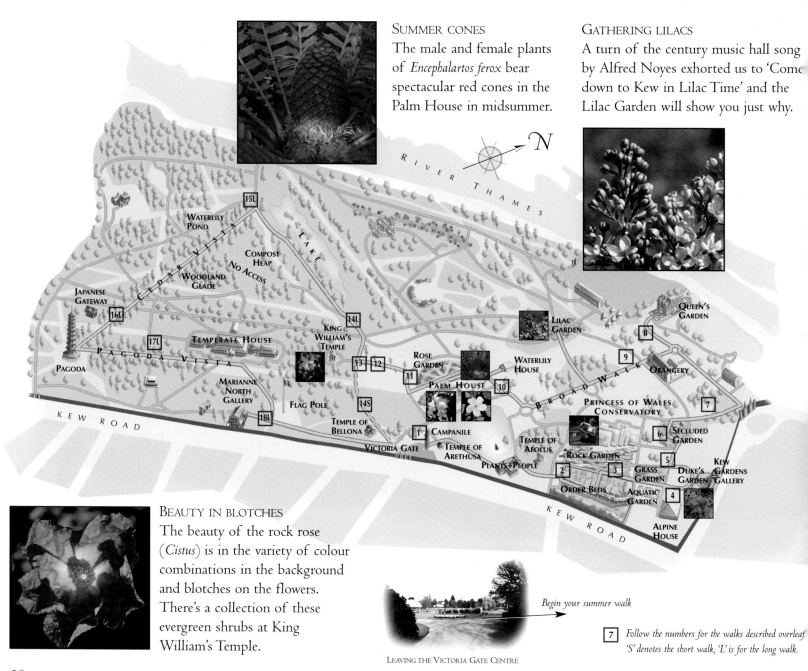

SUMMER CONES
The male and female plants of *Encephalartos ferox* bear spectacular red cones in the Palm House in midsummer.

GATHERING LILACS
A turn of the century music hall song by Alfred Noyes exhorted us to 'Come down to Kew in Lilac Time' and the Lilac Garden will show you just why.

N

RIVER THAMES

LAKE

15L

WATERLILY POND

COMPOST HEAP
No Access

CEDAR VISTA

WOODLAND GLADE

JAPANESE GATEWAY

16L

TEMPERATE HOUSE

17L

PAGODA VISTA

PAGODA

MARIANNE NORTH GALLERY

KING WILLIAM'S TEMPLE

14L

13   12

11

ROSE GARDEN

LILAC GARDEN

QUEEN'S GARDEN

8

9

WATERLILY HOUSE

ORANGERY

BROAD WALK

PALM HOUSE

10

PRINCESS OF WALES CONSERVATORY

7

FLAG POLE

14S

18L

TEMPLE OF BELLONA

VICTORIA GATE

1   CAMPANILE

TEMPLE OF ARETHUSA

PLANTS+PEOPLE

TEMPLE OF AEOLUS

ROCK GARDEN

2   3

ORDER BEDS

GRASS GARDEN

AQUATIC GARDEN

5

DUKE'S GARDEN

6   SECLUDED GARDEN

KEW GARDENS GALLERY

4

ALPINE HOUSE

KEW ROAD

KEW ROAD

BEAUTY IN BLOTCHES
The beauty of the rock rose (*Cistus*) is in the variety of colour combinations in the background and blotches on the flowers. There's a collection of these evergreen shrubs at King William's Temple.

Begin your summer walk

LEAVING THE VICTORIA GATE CENTRE

7 *Follow the numbers for the walks described overleaf 'S' denotes the short walk, 'L' is for the long walk.*

Summer at Kew

easons and flowering times can vary by up to three weeks so the periods below are only approximate.
or up-to-date details of flowering, please call 020 8332 5655 or visit the website at www.kew.org

rom June to early September, the Gardens are in full bloom. Early on, the Lilac Garden is a picture, while the Secluded Garden,
ydrangeas, hibiscus and Queen's Garden make stunning, longer-lasting shows.

Magnificent Indian horse chestnuts display their huge candles of bloom, and the Rose Garden and Grass Garden are 'musts' for
many visitors. Summer scents fill the air from the special selection of plants around King William's Temple. You'll find some
lever ideas in the Gravel Garden sponsored by Thames Water - it's in the Duke's Garden.

he map shows you where the summer displays are, and if you would like to try a favourite summer walk, turn to the next page.

DRUNK WITH PLEASURE
Hibiscus - there are some in the
Palm House - are wonderfully showy,
though the flowers are usually short-
lived. If you like drinking herbal teas,
look at the ingredients - you'll find
hibiscus prominent.

SUMMER SCENTS
The sweet perfume of
frangipani (*Plumeria rubra*)
and white spider lilies
(*Hymenocallis*) can fill the air
in the Palm House.

GIANTS
Giant waterlilies in the Princess of
Wales Conservatory and the Waterlily
House are as amazing now as they were
to the early Victorians when the first
specimens arrived here.

LAVENDER PINK, LAVENDER BLUE
The Lavender Trail at the Duke's
Garden shows the wonderful
variety of this popular plant,
and includes French lavender
(*Lavandula stoechas*) with its
attractive ear tufts.

Summer Walks

You can take a long or a short version of this walk. At a gentle pace, stopping to look at plants, but not lingering, the short walk takes about an hour to an hour and a half; the long walk about about an hour longer, starting and ending at the Victoria Gate Centre. You can follow the walk, which is on both paths and grass, from the description below and/or from the summer map on the previous page.

Sunflower

Peony

Waterlily

1 Leave the Visitor Centre, pass the Campanile, turn right at the Temple of Arethusa and make your way round the Pond to the Plants+People Exhibition. If you have time, look in to see just how important plants are to our lives. Turn sharp right at the end of the building and with the Temple of Aeolus on its hillock to the left, follow the path to the peony beds.

2 Past the peonies are the Order Beds, where related plants are grouped together in a fascinating and colourful parade.

3 In this area, there are several gardens handily next to each other. Leave the Order Beds by the centre left exit and you are faced with the colourful Rock Garden. Further on, to the right, the Aquatic Garden has superb waterlilies and marginal plants. There are miniatures to enjoy later in the Alpine House.

4 Turning right out of the Alpine House, there's the Grass Garden, with the Kew Gardens Gallery and the Duke's Garden next door. Here, there's the sweetly-scented Lavender Trail and the Gravel Garden, with lots of ideas for plants that need very little water.

5 Turn right out of Duke's Garden and on the left there's a path to the Princess of Wales Conservatory, worth a detour if you have time. There's a seasonal display where you enter and a magnificent giant waterlily should be in full flower in the centre.

6 Continue along the path to the huge stone pine tree. Opposite is a sign leading into the Secluded Garden, with plants to stimulate all the senses, a conservatory and a bamboo tunnel.

Go through the Secluded Garden and turn right to the Main Gate, where you turn left along a path lined with magnificent Indian horse chestnut trees, with candles of flowers proud on their branches.

Pass the rear of the Orangery, go ahead at the floral roundabout to the formal Queen's Garden behind Kew Palace, with a wonderful collection of plants popular in the 17th century and the splendid Laburnum Arch.

Come back to the Orangery, where you might stop for something to eat and drink. Go up the Broad Walk and about half way, in early summer specially, turn right for a detour visit to the Lilac Garden.

10 Come back to the Broad Walk, turn right and head right at the roundabout for the Palm House. Turn right into the Waterlily House to see not only a giant waterlily, but loofahs, papyrus and the sacred lotus.

11 Inside and either side of the Palm House are joys. There's summer bedding on the Pond side and a vast display of roses on the other. Enjoy any or all of them, then take the path away from the roses in the direction of the Temperate House.

12 Soon, there's a crossroads in front of King William's Temple, with its specially planted collection of highly-scented Mediterranean style shrubs, herbs and other plants - a feast for all your senses.

13 *Short walk or long walk?*
Here is where you make your decision. For the short walk - you've almost completed it by now, with only about ten minutes to go - follow the sign to Victoria Gate. For the long walk, (around an hour more back to the Victoria Gate Centre) follow the signpost to the Lake.

Short walk

14S Your way back goes past the Temple of Bellona straight down to the Victoria Gate Centre where you started this summer day here in Kew Gardens.

Long walk

14L Where five paths meet, continue virtually straight ahead to the Lake, taking the right hand path to keep by the lakeside. Just over halfway along, you'll find a viewing platform to one of the biggest compost heaps in Britain. Recycling is very important at Kew.

15L Continue to the head of the Lake and bear round sharp left to head down the grass walk of Cedar Vista. On the right, the Waterlily Pond is very attractive in summer and just past it on the left, the seclusion of the Woodland Glade makes a welcome diversion.

short walk   long walk

16L Carry on down Cedar Vista over several paths to the tranquillity of the Japanese Gateway and Landscape on the right and then, just ahead, the Pagoda reaches up to its full ornate height. There's a fragrant planting of philadelphus by the Pagoda, filling the air with orange blossom scent.

17L Turn left and walk the length of the Pagoda Vista - don't forget to look behind you to appreciate the view. Just past the centre steps to the Temperate House on your left, fork right to pass the impressive Flagpole.

18L At the T-junction past the Flagpole, turning right leads to the Marianne North Gallery with its collection of flower paintings; or turn left and the path leads back to the Victoria Gate Centre.

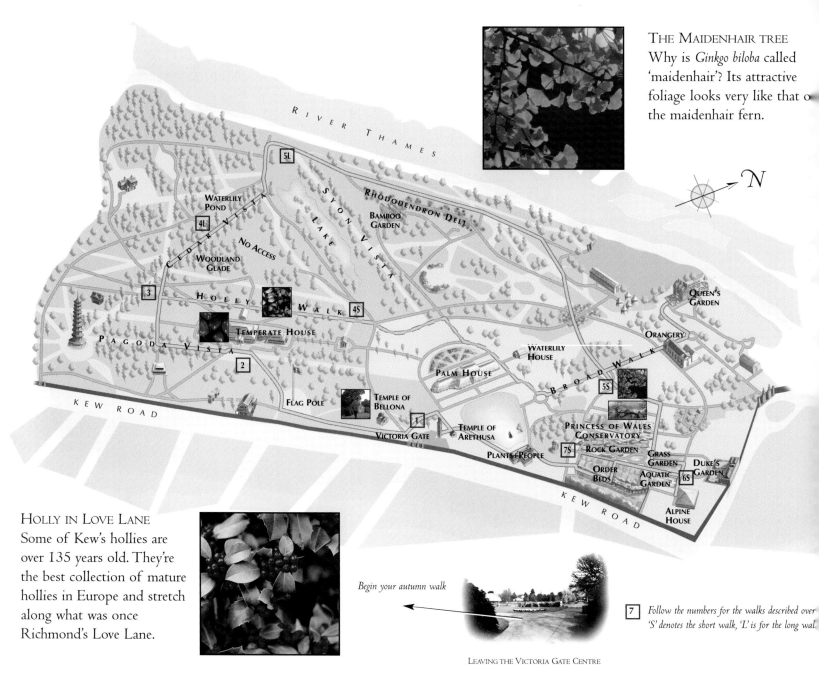

THE MAIDENHAIR TREE
Why is *Ginkgo biloba* called 'maidenhair'? Its attractive foliage looks very like that o the maidenhair fern.

N

RIVER THAMES

5L

WATERLILY POND

4L

SYON VISTA

RHODODENDRON DELL

BAMBOO GARDEN

CEDAR VISTA

No Access

WOODLAND GLADE

LAKE

3

H O L L Y   W A L K

4S

QUEEN'S GARDEN

P A G O D A   V I S T A

TEMPERATE HOUSE

ORANGERY

WATERLILY HOUSE

2

PALM HOUSE

BROAD WALK

5S

FLAG POLE

TEMPLE OF BELLONA

1

PRINCESS OF WALES CONSERVATORY

VICTORIA GATE

TEMPLE OF ARETHUSA

7S

ROCK GARDEN

GRASS GARDEN

DUKE'S GARDEN

PLANTS+PEOPLE

ORDER BEDS

AQUATIC GARDEN

6S

KEW ROAD

ALPINE HOUSE

KEW ROAD

HOLLY IN LOVE LANE
Some of Kew's hollies are over 135 years old. They're the best collection of mature hollies in Europe and stretch along what was once Richmond's Love Lane.

Begin your autumn walk

7 *Follow the numbers for the walks described over 'S' denotes the short walk, 'L' is for the long wal*

LEAVING THE VICTORIA GATE CENTRE

14

Autumn at Kew

seasons and flowering times can vary by up to three weeks so the periods below are only approximate.
For up-to-date details of flowering, please call 020 8332 5655 or visit the website at www.kew.org

September and October and, so variable are our seasons nowadays, probably well into November, bring in the poetic 'season of mists and mellow fruitfulness'. Autumn colour, as deciduous trees shut down their leaf activity, is at its most striking. Berries ripen and some trees start their bark colour changes too.

There's still more colour with autumn crocus, hardy cyclamens and belladonna lilies, while the Grass Garden never ceases to fascinate with its huge variety of plants, ranging from the highly decorative ornamental grasses to the most useful cereal crops. If ever a plant family supported mankind, it's the grasses. Just three cereals - maize, wheat and rice - provide nearly two-thirds of the calories and half the protein consumed by the world's population.

The Woodland Glade and the Duke's Garden are also thoroughly rewarding to visit at this time of year.

SMOKE, BUT NO FIRE
The smoke bush (*Cotinus coggygria*) is famous for its hazy covering of feathery flowers that gives it its name. Its splendid autumn colours are almost luminous.

AN ANCIENT INHABITANT
This splendidly gnarled Japanese pagoda tree (*Sophora japonica*) is one of Kew's oldest trees, having been brought here in 1762.

HOT STUFF
Chillies (*Capsicum*), shown here, are fruiting in the Temperate House, along with citrus fruits and the curious tree tomatoes.

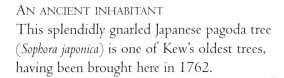

Autumn Walks

There are long and short versions of this walk, which starts and ends at the Victoria Gate Centre. The short walk can take between 90 minutes and two and a half hours, depending on how much time you spend in the glasshouses and detours. The long walk takes about an hour longer. You can follow the walks, which are on both paths and grass, from the description below and/or from the autumn map on the previous page.

BLAZING MAPLES
A touch of America's eastern seaboard comes to Kew with a blaze of 'fall colour'.

THE PAGODA
The Pagoda was built for Princess Augusta, who founded the botanic garden at Kew in 1759.

1 From the Visitor Centre, turn left at the Palm House Pond and go past the gate itself to the path parallel to Kew Road, where the smoke bush is by the Temple of Bellona. Continue along the path to just past the huge Flagpole, where you turn right and walk through a blaze of autumn colour among the maples towards the Temperate House.

2 Before you reach it, turn left on to the grass of Pagoda Vista, through more glorious autumn colour. Turn right at the first path (away from the Pavilion Restaurant), and go past the end of the Temperate House to a crossing.

SPECTACULAR
SPINDLE TREES
Spindle trees (*Euonymus*) are grown for the spectacular colours of their autumn fruits, in which the seeds are just as brightly coloured. The evergreen varieties are good seaside plants.

long walk

short walk

Short walk or long walk?

Here is where you make your decision. For the short walk (one or two hours back to the Victoria Gate Centre, depending on the stops you make), turn right at the signpost to the Palm House and Evolution House. For the long walk (about another hour longer), continue straight up, over the grass, to where the broad spread of Cedar Vista forks off to the right.

Short walk

S It's burgeoning berries all the way as you stroll parallel to the Temperate House along Holly Walk. At a five-way junction, fork right and then turn right on the path through the Rose Garden and then between the Palm and Waterlily Houses. Carry on to the roundabout and turn left up the Broad Walk towards the Orangery. Here, you can make a detour to the Orangery for light refreshments and, if you have the time (about an extra 20-30 minutes), you could see the beautiful autumn-flowering cyclamen under the pleached hornbeams in the Queen's Garden behind Kew Palace.

5S Otherwise, halfway down the Broad Walk turn off towards the Princess of Wales Conservatory and the Japanese pagoda tree is on the right. Turn right just before the wisteria on an old pergola and go past the Princess of Wales Conservatory. Turn left into the Grass Garden to see just how large and useful a family it is, from ornamentals to cereals.

6S There are signs to the nearby Alpine House, glowing with autumn bulbs. Come back past the Aquatic Garden to the path between a wall and the Rock Garden. Halfway along the wall, go into the Order Beds, which show just how attractive serried ranks of seed heads can look.

7S Now head towards Museum No I and the Plants+People Exhibition, which is really worth while seeing, so try to make the time. To end your autumn walk, continue round the Pond opposite the Palm House and turn left at the Temple of Arethusa to the Victoria Gate Centre.

Long walk

4L From 3 above, you have continued over the grass to fork right into Cedar Vista, walking through glorious autumn colour, past the Waterlily Pond, past the head of the Lake, heading for the Thames. Don't forget to look back for the view. When you reach the river and the sight of Syon House, turn right along the path.

5L Fork left towards Brentford Gate, passing the Bamboo Garden and Rhododendron Dell on the right. Fork right away from Brentford Gate and go straight down to the Broad Walk. There, a left turn to the Orangery would bring you some light refreshments. And if you have a little extra time (about 20-30 minutes), you could see the beautiful autumn-flowering cyclamen in the Queen's Garden behind Kew Palace. Otherwise, cross straight over to join up with the short walk route at 5S.

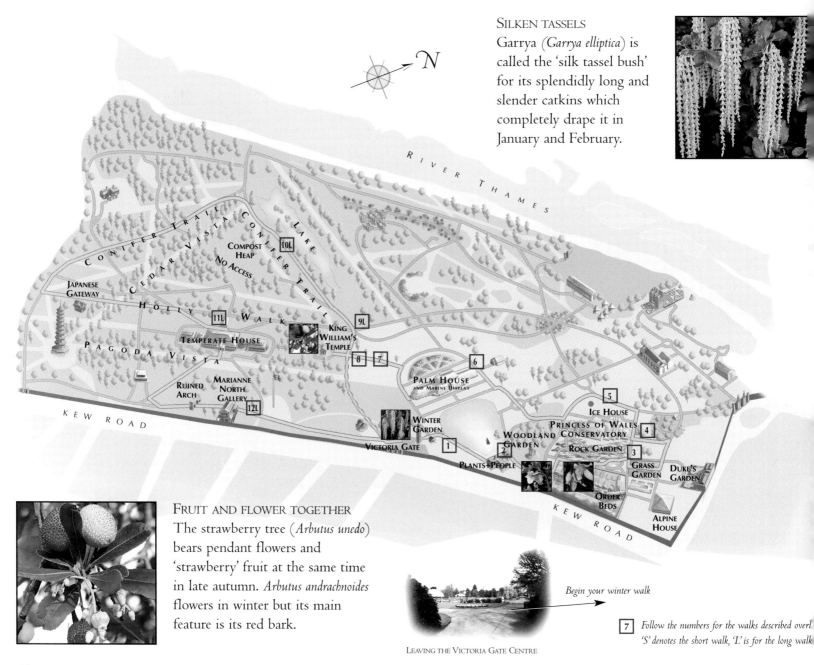

SILKEN TASSELS
Garrya (*Garrya elliptica*) is called the 'silk tassel bush' for its splendidly long and slender catkins which completely drape it in January and February.

R I V E R   T H A M E S

CONIFER TRAIL

CEDAR VISTA

CONIFER TRAIL

LAKE

10L

COMPOST HEAP

No Access

JAPANESE GATEWAY

HOLLY WALK

11L

TEMPERATE HOUSE

KING WILLIAM'S TEMPLE

9L

PAGODA VISTA

8   7

6

RUINED ARCH

MARIANNE NORTH GALLERY

12L

PALM HOUSE
AND MARINE DISPLAY

5

ICE HOUSE

WINTER GARDEN

PRINCESS OF WALES

4

VICTORIA GATE

1

WOODLAND GARDEN

CONSERVATORY

ROCK GARDEN

3

KEW ROAD

PLANTS + PEOPLE

2

GRASS GARDEN

DUKE'S GARDEN

ORDER BEDS

KEW ROAD

ALPINE HOUSE

FRUIT AND FLOWER TOGETHER
The strawberry tree (*Arbutus unedo*) bears pendant flowers and 'strawberry' fruit at the same time in late autumn. *Arbutus andrachnoides* flowers in winter but its main feature is its red bark.

LEAVING THE VICTORIA GATE CENTRE

Begin your winter walk

7 *Follow the numbers for the walks described overl*
'S' denotes the short walk, 'L' is for the long walk

18

Winter at Kew

easons and flowering times can vary by up to three weeks so the periods below are only approximate. or up-to-date details of flowering, please call 020 8332 5655 or visit the website at www.kew.org

November right round to February - and there's more to see in the Gardens than you might think. At the end of the ear, there is winter bark to look out for; the pretty winter-flowering cherry and the simultaneous flowers and trawberry-like fruit of the strawberry tree. Try Holly Walk to ease you into the festive spirit.

he New Year brings winter-flowering shrubs, such as wintersweet and witch hazel, with heady scents and a mass of owers, all round the Ice House; hellebores in the Winter Garden; and a great show of snowdrops by the Ruined Arch nd in the Rock Garden.

's a comforting thought, visiting Kew in the depths of winter, that you can always warm up in one of the plant ouses and imagine you have escaped to the lush tropics.

HIDDEN BEAUTY
Low down near the ground, the nodding flowers of the hellebores are hiding their beauty.
The Christmas rose (*Helleborus niger*) appears around mid-winter.

A LITTLE LIVERISH?
Clematis cirrhosa is one of the few evergreen clematis.
Its late winter flowers are speckled inside and look like a diseased liver - hence *cirrhosa*.

KEW FOR CHRISTMAS TREES
Wakehurst Place, Kew's sister garden in the beautiful High Sussex Weald, manages woodland traditionally and practically. It produces superb quality Christmas trees, available for sale at the Victoria Gate Centre. All funds raised go to support Kew's work.

Winter Walks

You can take a long or a short version of this walk. At a gentle pace, the short walk takes about an hour, the long walk about two hours, starting and ending at the Victoria Gate Centre. You can follow the walk, which is on both paths and grass, from the description below and/or from the winter map on the previous page.

BEAUTIFUL BARK
Birch trees are known for their beautiful bark, which varies enormously in colour. This is silver birch (*Betula pendula*).

HARBINGERS OF SPRING
It's a sure sign that spring is on its way when the tough pointed buds of snowdrops (*Galanthus*) push their way through hard ground and open their demure little flowers.

1 There's a display of winter flowers immediately on the left on leaving the Visitor Centre. After seeing it, go to the right round the Palm House Pond, along a glorious row of winter-flowering viburnum to the Plants+ People Exhibition, which is well worth a visit.

2 Turn right at the end of the building, and pass the Temple of Aeolus, where you will find flowering hellebores, daphne and snowdrops in the Woodland Garden. Follow the path round left, past the Order Beds and, after the wall, turn right into the Rock Garden, taking its centre path.

3 Taking the little tunnel in the Rock Garden brings you out near the Grass Garden (on the right) with some sculptural seed heads on view. Through the grasses to the path by the Duke's Garden where you'll find wintersweet. Turn left and go up the path to the stone pine and turn left again to the Princess of Wales Conservatory.

On turning right at the Conservatory
here's a paper-bark maple on the
corner, with stunning bark - dark brown
peeling off to reveal layers of vibrant
orange beneath.

5 Go up to the T-junction, turn left
past the Japanese pagoda tree and keep
left for the Ice House, with its winter
garden of fragrant flowers. Continuing
round, turn right for the roundabout
and over it to the Palm House.
The Pond outside usually has a number
of ornamental wildfowl preening
themselves at the sight of a visitor.

6 Go through the lush warmth of the
Palm House, taking in the Marine
Display in the basement for a fascinating
glimpse of four marine environments;
and out past the oldest pot plant in the
world, through the far (South) door
and, on leaving, turn right.

7 Take the first path left towards King
William's Temple, around which there
are strawberry trees on the Lake side
and the collection of witch hazels
(in bloom from December to February)
on the other.

8 *Short walk or long walk?*
Here is where you make your
decision. For the short walk, simply
follow the signposts to Victoria Gate
Centre, which is very close.

Long walk

9L For the long walk (about an hour
more from here), follow the signpost to
the Lake. This is the start of the
Conifer Trail, with trees clearly marked,
exploring the rich variety of conifers
from around the world.

10L Take the right fork to the Lake,
on which you may well see some
interesting wildlife; and up past the
Compost Heap viewing platform.
At the head of the Lake, take the path
that forks left, still on the Conifer
Trail. Keep walking, following the signs
to Lion Gate and Pagoda, until you
turn left to pass the Japanese Gateway.
Keep straight ahead along the Holly
Walk until you fork right and go in
through the middle doors of the
Temperate House.

short walk ← → long walk

11L Inside the Temperate House,
you'll find the spectacular bird of
paradise flowers in full bloom, along
with banksias and sub-tropical
rhododendrons.

12L Leave by the middle doors on the
Kew Road side and take the right hand
path, turning left at the far end to the
Ruined Arch and a fine display of
hellebores. Continue on past the
Marianne North Gallery - it is worth
your while to see the eye-opening
collection of her flower paintings -
and on a few more yards to the
Victoria Gate Centre where you started
this winter walk.

The Palm House

Palms are second only to grasses in their importance to people. About 70% of all palm species are found in tropical rainforests, one of the most threatened habitats on earth. The Palm House creates conditions similar to tropical rainforest; around a quarter of the palms planted here are threatened in the wild, as are more than half of the cycads, the 'living fossils' of the tropics.

The Palm House also contains many plants of great economic significance, grown for their yields of fruits, timber, spices, fibres, perfumes and medicines. Plants are grouped together in geographical areas, except in the centre, where the tallest specimens need the extra height of the dome.

The Marine Display in the basement recreates four important marine habitats, complete with fish, corals and other sea creatures, and shows the importance of marine plants.

THE WORLD'S SMELLIEST FRUIT

The legendary durian has a sublime taste, but a foul smell - the experience has been described as 'Like eating custard in a sewer.'

THE WORLD'S FASTEST-GROWING PLANTS

Two species of giant bamboo can grow 45 cm (18 ins) in 24 hours and can reach maximum heights of around 25 m (82 ft). They are used for scaffolding and paper production.

AFRICA
South Wing

This vast continent has very few palm species, but one - the African oil palm (*Elaeis guineensis*) - is the most important oil-producing plantation palm in the tropics. Coffee bushes (*Coffea*), which often produce berries in the Palm House; and the Madagascar periwinkle (*Catharanthus roseus*) from which anti-leukemia drugs were developed, are valuable plants which originated in Africa.

Madagascar and other islands off Africa are richer in palms and Kew is proud of its rare triangle palm (*Dypsis decaryi*) and the double coconut palm (*Lodoicea maldivica*) from the Seychelles, which bears a bizarre seed, the largest in the world.

South Africa is rich in cycads (shown below) - the 'living fossils' of the plant world - and one of Kew's specimens, *Encephalartos altensteinii*, is the world's oldest pot-plant having been brought here in 1775. Nearby are the male and female plants of *Encephalartos ferox*, which bear spectacular red cones in midsummer.

THE AMERICAS
Centre Transept

The Victorians concentrated on palms from the Americas, the world's richest rainforest habitat. Caribbean palms and rare Mexican cycads have their own areas and visitors often recognise their own houseplants in some of the *Chamaedorea* palms.

Many vitally important economic specimens are planted here, including cocoa, rubber, bananas, papaya, soursop, cherimoya and mammee-apple. The Mexican yam (*Dioscorea macrostachya*) is important medicinally, as it was used to develop the contraceptive pill and *Smilax utilis* is interesting because the tonic drink sarsaparilla is made from its roots. Rare timbers include mahogany and the Caribbean lignum vitæ.

The parrot flowers (*Heliconia*) (shown below) and the hybrid rose of Venezuela (*Brownea*) often display splashes of scarlet and in summer, the sweet scents of frangipani (*Plumeria rubra*) and white spider lilies (*Hymenocallis*) can fill the air.

W

Temperate House
and Lake

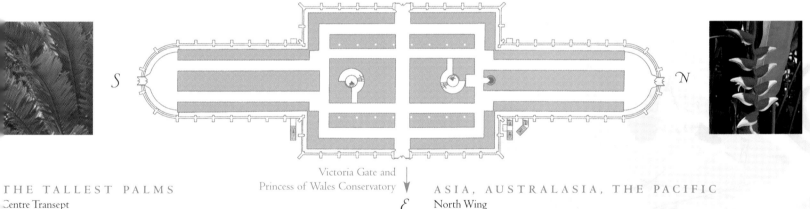

S

N

Victoria Gate and
Princess of Wales Conservatory

E

THE TALLEST PALMS
Centre Transept

What dictates a planting position under the great central dome of the Palm House is not geography, but sheer height, which cannot be reduced without killing the growing point, or 'heart' of the plant. The many-stemmed peach palm (*Bactris gasipaes*) is often felled for its edible heart - 'coeur de palmier'.

Also here are the babassu (*Attalea speciosa*), used in many ways in central South America; the fast-growing queen palm (*Syagrus romanzoffiana*), so popular with landscapers; the American oil palm (*Elaeis oleifera*); the rare *Borassodendron borneense* from Borneo and the pantropical coconut palm (*Cocos nucifera*) which actually fruits at Kew.

ASIA, AUSTRALASIA, THE PACIFIC
North Wing

This area of the world is home to the greatest diversity in the palm family and Kew has a rich collection, including many shade-loving 'understorey' specimens, dwarf palms and climbing rattans, from which most 'cane' furniture is made.

Many Asian fruit trees are planted here. Some are fairly familiar to us - lychee, mango and starfruit. More unusual are breadfruit, jackfruit, mangosteen and Indonesia's legendary durian, the 'King of Fruit'. Sugar cane grows well in here, and common spices, such as ginger, pepper and cardamom, are seen here as growing plants.

The jade vine (*Strongylodon macrobotrys*) is one of the Palm House's most notable plants, with enormous wisteria-like flowers in iridescent jade green. Finally, in the apse end, there's a selection of potted palms with their characteristic 'feather' or 'fan' leaves.

The Palm House

PLANTING AND CONSERVATION

The Palm House represents one habitat - tropical rainforest. The plantings simulate its multi-layered nature with canopy palms and other trees, climbers and epiphytes and then down to the shorter understorey plants and dwarf palms. The cycads here are solely from rainforests.

Many of the plants in this collection are endangered in the wild; some are even extinct. Their natural habitats are being destroyed by clearing for agriculture, mining, or logging. Scientists at Kew are deeply involved in surveys and studies of palms and other rainforest species to assess the diversity of habitats and to develop methods for the sustainable growth and harvesting of these plants.

All life depends on plants. If left unchecked, the current rate of destruction of the world's rainforests will see the total loss of this environment by the middle of the next century, together with its peoples, its vast untapped potential for crops and medicines, and its vital moderating effect on the earth's climate.

The Palm House, then, is more than just a collection to gaze at and wonder. It is an invaluable world resource.

RAINFOREST PLANTS IN THE WORLD ECONOMY

The Palm House collection contains many plants of significant economic importance, and one of Kew's roles is research into many of the factors that make for sustainable cropping.

Here are some examples to look for:-

RUBBER TREE
(*Hevea brasiliensis*)

Natural rubber has unique properties, making it important for special uses, from robust space shuttle tyres to delicate contraceptives. In 1876, Kew received 70,000 seeds collected from the tree's native Amazonian Brazil. Only 2,800 germinated, but from them, the seedlings sent to Sri Lanka and Malaysia flourished and started their rubber industries.

Rubber on tap
The white latex that flows in the inner bark of the rubber tree is tapped by a series of cuts.

AFRICAN OIL PALM
(*Elaeis guineensis*)

Native to tropical Africa, this, the most productive oil-producing tropical plant, is grown in plantations throughout the world's humid tropics. Palm oil pressed from the orange flesh makes soap, candles and some edible products. Oil from the stone's hard white kernel is also used for edible oils and fats, soaps and detergents. In Africa, the sap is tapped for palm wine, and the leaves and trunk help make houses.

COCOA (*Theobroma cacao*)
The Aztecs called it 'Food of the Gods', hence its scientific name deriving from 'theos' (gods) and 'bromos' (food). Originally a bitter beverage reserved for Aztec high society, the Spanish added sugar and vanilla to create its modern taste.

GIANT BAMBOO
(*Gigantochloa verticillata*)

Bamboos are in the grass family and are known as 'friend of the people' in China and 'wood of the poor' in India. Giant bamboo is highly versatile, used in house construction and paper-making, while the young shoots are a table delicacy. However, land clearance for agriculture has resulted in the total destruction of many natural habitats of bamboo.

PEPPER (*Piper nigrum*)

The fruits of this woody climber, native to India, are the familiar peppercorns, yielding the world's most important spice. Black pepper comes from grinding the whole dried peppercorn; for white pepper, the outer husk is removed. Pepper was first used as a cooking spice in India; then came to Europe in the Middle Ages to flavour and cure meat. It was also used with other spices to mask the taste of bad food.

MADAGASCAR PERIWINKLE
(*Catharanthus roseus*)

Traditionally used in folk remedies for digestive complaints and diabetes, this pretty ornamental (shown far left) is recognised as important in the fight against cancer. Two of its six especially useful alkaloids can be used to treat leukaemia and Hodgkin's Disease. Commonly cultivated, it is now rare in the wild as deforestation destroys its habitat and that of other potentially useful relatives.

COFFEE (*Coffea*)

Coffee was first used as a paste of beans and oil, chewed for the caffeine effect, but by the 15th century people were roasting beans to produce a drink. Originally African, most of the world's coffee now comes from Latin America. Arabica beans (*Coffea arabica*) make quality coffee, while the robusta (*Coffea canephora*) is a better commercial crop generally used for instant coffee.

COCONUT
(*Cocos nucifera*)

The origin of the most familiar tropical palm is probably in the islands of the western Pacific and eastern Indian oceans, spreading by ocean currents and human planting. Every part of the tree is used; the trunk for timber, leaves provide thatch, baskets and brooms; while the nut provides food, drink and kernel oil from inside and coir fibre and garden mulch from the outside.

SUGAR CANE (*Saccharum officinarum*)

Another invaluable grass, sugar cane originated in New Guinea, where ancient people used the stem for chewing. Today, raw cane sugar is a major world commodity and by-products such as molasses and bagasse (used for fuel) are valuable, too. Fuel alcohol produced from sugar is used in 50% of all cars in Brazil - a cheap, renewable and less polluting tankful.

PEPPERCORN RENT

Peppercorns were once so expensive that rents were paid in them - hence peppercorn rent. Today, it means just a token payment.

25

The Palm House

THE ICON OF KEW

Built 1844-48 by Richard Turner to Decimus Burton's designs, the Palm House is Kew's most recognisable building, having gained iconic status as the world's most important surviving Victorian glass and iron structure.

BORROWED TECHNOLOGY

While the thinking was Burton's, the 'doing' - the extraordinary engineering and construction work - was very much Richard Turner's. The technology was borrowed from shipbuilding and the design is essentially an upturned hull. The unprecedented use of light but strong wrought iron 'ship's beams' made the great open span possible.

MARRYING FORM AND FUNCTION

The Palm House was built for the exotic palms being collected and introduced to Europe in early Victorian times. The elegant design with its unobstructed space for the spreading crowns of the tall palms was a perfect marriage of form and function.

Burton chose the site so that his building would be reflected in the Pond to the east. Two tree-lined vistas - Pagoda Vista and Syon Vista - landscaped by William Nesfield, radiate from this focal point of the Gardens.

CAMPANILE

Originally, the boilers were in the Palm House basement, heating water pipes under iron gratings on which the plants stood in great teak tubs, or in clay pots on benches. The smoke from the boilers was led away through pipes in a tunnel to an elegant Italianate campanile smoke stack 150 m (490 ft) away. However, the boiler room was constantly flooded, and some parts of the Palm House were too cold.

By the early 1950s, over a hundred years of external weathering, together with high temperature and humidity inside, had taken their toll. Restoration was long overdue.

THE WORLD'S OLDEST POT-PLANT

This cycad, *Encephalartos altensteinii*, was brought to Kew in 1775 and typifies the Palm House's original arrangement of plants displayed in pots. It needed special care when moved for the restoration in the 1980s.

The restorations

The first restoration was in 1955-57, when glazing bars were cleaned and realigned and the house completely reglazed. New beds were built and the plants simply moved around to accommodate the works. The boilers were converted to oil and moved to a site behind the Campanile, using the tunnel to take hot water to the heating system. A later conversion to dual-fuel (oil or gas) boilers has resulted in gas being the standard fuel.

Palms on the move

The second restoration, 1984-88, was much more comprehensive after major work was found to be vital, for both the building and the heating system.

For the first time in its history, the Palm House was completely emptied. Most palms were 'heeled in' in temporary glasshouses, but some were too large, so were cut down and made into specimens for the Herbarium and Museum.

Grade I listed building

The Palm House is a world-famous Grade I listed building. It was dismantled entirely, restored and rebuilt, with parts replaced like for like. Burton and Turner were at the leading edge of their glazing technology, but standards today are vastly superior. Toughened safety glass is held by ten miles of glazing bars made of modern stainless steel, but to exactly the same section as the originals.

The floor layout was revised to allow planting in beds, rather than pots, which made room for wider paths and seats for visitors. The basement was enlarged to house staff facilities and the new Marine Display.

The second restoration took as long to complete as the original house took to build. Replanting was completed in mid-August 1989 and H.M. Queen Elizabeth the Queen Mother officially reopened the Palm House on 6 November 1990.

The Marine Display

All life originated in the sea. Today, millions of years later, life still depends on the most simple marine plants - the algae. Algae, which include all seaweeds, provide half of the world's oxygen supplies and absorb vast amounts of carbon dioxide. As Sir David Attenborough put it, "Without algae, there would be no life on earth, the seas would be sterile and the land would be uncolonised."

The Marine Display was created in the basement of the Palm House during its last restoration. It emphasises the importance of marine plants and, through displays in 19 tanks, recreates four major marine habitats.

EAT AND BE EATEN

Algae are a vital first link in the ocean's food chain. They are also largely unexploited by man, but that situation is changing. Japanese nori and Welsh laverbread are well-established foods. Seaweed has been widely used as land fertiliser and animal fodder in coastal communities, too. Today, algal products include a variety of gels, such as agar, alginates and carrageenan; used in ice cream, growing media for microbial culture, paints and very effective wound dressings.

Seaweed

CORAL REEFS are among the most unique, complex and productive habitats on the planet. Reef-building corals are animals - coral polyps - most of which obtain some of their nutrients from minute algae in the tissues. The polyps extract calcium from seawater and excrete it to form their chalky external skeletons, which create the reef.

Human intervention, such as industrial scale prawn fishing and even uncontrolled tourism, together with natural disasters, can threaten the fine balance of these often fragile ecosystems.

ESTUARIES AND SALT MARSHES, where rivers meet the sea, are fertile and productive tracts with their own communities of hardy and vigorous 'pioneer' plants. Pioneer plants stabilise mud and silt, raising the mud level and eventually, as other species arrive and the cycle continues, dry land appears.

MANGROVE SWAMPS are the tropical equivalents of salt marshes and have evolved their own flora and fauna for the local conditions. Estuaries, salt marshes and mangrove swamps, by their very nature

Tube Coral

positioned between land and sea, are highly adaptable habitats of constant change and development. They provide vital nurseries for fish and other marine life.

ROCKY SHORELINES at the base of cliffs, of which the British Isles have many miles, are among the best habitats for highly productive populations of seaweeds. Different seaweeds are adapted to surviving in distinct zones with other plants and animals. The tidal regime - the depth and reach of the tides - together with the topography and geology of the shoreline, determine which seaweed thrives where.

LITTLE AND LARGE
Algae vary enormously in shape and size. The tiny, single-celled micro-algae (sometimes called phytoplankton), include the world's smallest plant, *Chlorella*, which is only 0.003 mm in diameter. Among the huge macro-algae is giant kelp (*Macrocystis*) which, at up to 100 metres in length, is among the world's largest plants.

Giant kelp

SEAHORSES AND SEX
It's difficult not to warm to seahorses for their distinctive looks, the elegant way they glide upright through the water, and the way they anchor themselves to seaweed with their prehensile tails. Their reproduction techniques are very different, too. The female lays her eggs in a pouch in the male, where they brood and hatch. For the first few days after hatching, the young take shelter in the male's pouch, returning at frequent intervals. Two European species, *Hippocampus hippocampus* and *Hippocampus ramulosus* (with a longer snout and a more prominent 'mane') are found from the Mediterranean up to warmer stretches of the English Channel.

Among the seahorses in the Marine Display are *Hippocampus ramulosus* which were native to our waters until the 1920s, when their eel-grass habitat started vanishing. They have recently re-established themselves around Weymouth in Dorset. Kew's seahorses generated some excitement when they started breeding, something they rarely do in captivity.

GREEN SCUM AND RED TIDES
Micro-algae as single cells are usually invisible to the naked eye, but occur in vast numbers as green scum on ponds and red tides on beaches and in reservoirs. Under a microscope, they show a huge variety of often very beautiful shapes. Blue-green algae (cyanobacteria) are the world's oldest plants, appearing some 2,000 million years ago.

WHY SEAWEEDS ARE DIFFERENT COLOURS
Seaweeds are divided into groups by colour - green, brown and red. Green seaweeds live in shallow waters up to 10 m deep. Brown algae can survive in water up to 30 m deep, while red algae can survive in water to a depth of 100 m. All algae need light for photo-synthesis, and each group contains different coloured pigments to absorb the available daylight at different depths.

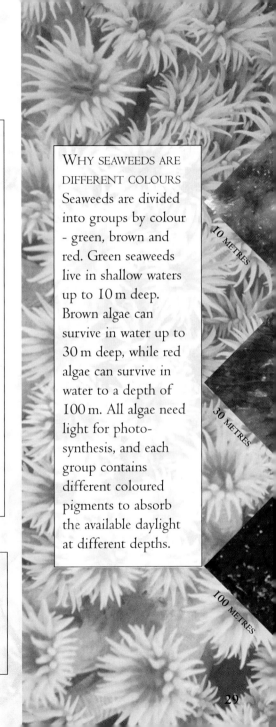

10 METRES

30 METRES

100 METRES

The Temperate House

THE LARGEST GLASSHOUSE AT KEW, FULL OF TENDER WOODY PLANTS FROM SUBTROPICAL AND WARM TEMPERATE REGIONS WORLDWIDE

Once the largest plant house in the world and now the world's largest surviving Victorian glass structure, the Temperate House is another of Decimus Burton's designs and yet another of Kew's 39 listed buildings. At 4,880 square metres, it is the largest public glasshouse at Kew, twice the size of the Palm House.

Tender woody plants from the world's temperate regions have always been a major part of the collection at Kew. In Victorian times, the intensity of collecting meant that the Orangery and many other houses quickly became vastly overcrowded so, in 1859, it was decided to build another major glasshouse to complement the Palm House.

Today, the planting has reverted to Decimus Burton's original geographical scheme and includes many unusual crop plants from warmer climates.

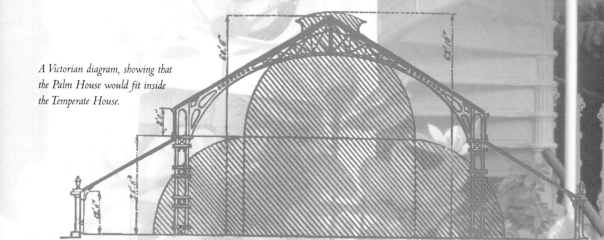

A Victorian diagram, showing that the Palm House would fit inside the Temperate House.

THE WORLD'S LARGEST INDOOR PLANT is the Chilean wine-palm (*Jubaea chilensis*) in the centre of the Temperate House, which is 16 m (52 ft) high - and still growing! It was grown from seed and there is a replacement nearby, ready for the time when this huge wine palm no longer fits into the roof space.

Tree fern

THE CENTRE contains many tall subtropical trees and palms as well as tree ferns.

THE NORTH OCTAGON holds plants from Australasia and the Pacific Islands.

King protea

THE SOUTH OCTAGON is home for South African heaths and proteas.

Metrosideros perforata

EVOLUTION HOUSE

Pagoda and Japanese Gateway

Palm House

THE SOUTH WING holds collections of African and Mediterranean plants.

Pavilion Restaurant and Lion Gate

Flagpole and Victoria Gate Centre

THE NORTH WING contains species from temperate Asia.

Rice paper plant

rd of Paradise flower

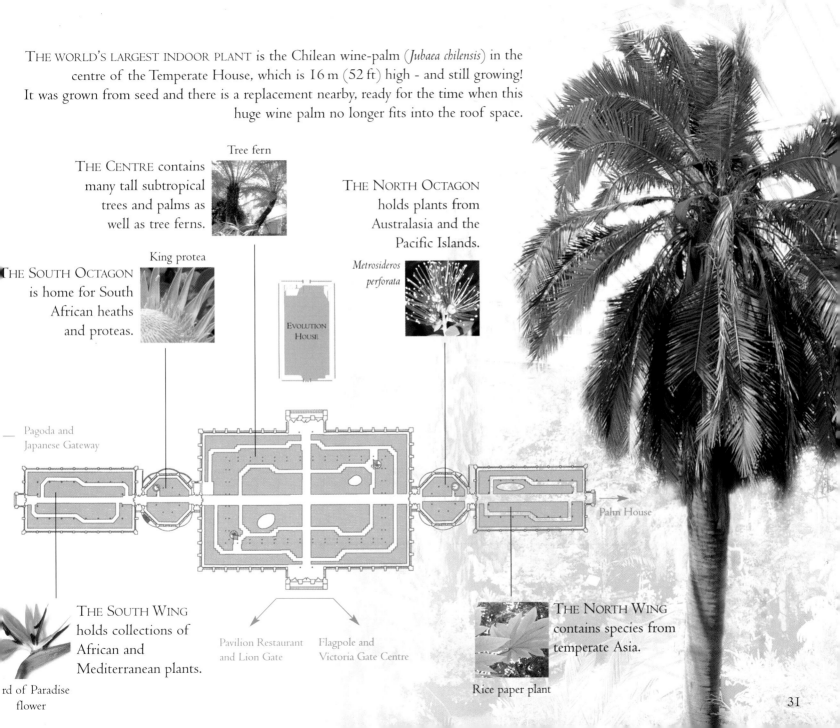

31

The Temperate House

TEMPERATE ZONES - TENDER WOODY PLANTS, MANY OF GROWING ECONOMIC IMPORTANCE

The plant collection in the Temperate House includes many spectacularly beautiful specimens that are deservedly admired, but it represents much more than that. Among the plants on display here are endangered island species being propagated for reintroduction to their native lands, such as *Hibiscus liliiflorus* from Rodrigues Island in the Indian Ocean.

There are also many plants of significant economic importance such as jojoba, a crop from arid lands which produces an oil that is often used in shampoos and cosmetics. It's interesting to see how oranges and lemons grow on their respective spiky trees, or how a cup of tea starts out as tender leaves from certain varieties of camellia bush.

The Temperate House has a notable collection of Australasian plants, such as grass trees; the delightful 'kangaroos paws' (so called for the shape of its flowers), and a fine array of banksias, named after Joseph Banks, who collected them and who is so intimately connected with Kew.

THE RAREST PLANT AT KEW
A cycad, *Encephalartos woodii*, was presented to Kew by the Natal National Park and is not only the rarest plant in the Gardens, but possibly the last surviving specimen in the world. All cycads bear male and female (seed) cones on different plants. As the one at Kew is a lone male, what the seed cones look like will never be known.

FLOWERS AFTER 160 YEARS
This king protea (*Protea cynaroides*) from the Cape seems to have relished the conditions after the 1980 restoration as it bloomed in 1986 after a gap of exactly 160 years and has produced flowers every year since then.

'G & T' TO LIFE-SAVER
From the bark of the cinchona tree comes quinine, famously used as a flavouring in Indian Tonic Water and taken world wide as a life-saving drug to counter malaria.

33

The Temperate House

In the mid-nineteenth century, the need for a large temperate greenhouse had become overwhelming, as the collection of tender woody plants had become so large. In 1859, the Government allocated £10,000 to build the Temperate House and directed Decimus Burton to prepare designs for this 'long-desiderated' conservatory. The Treasury called a halt when the account from Messrs Cubitt & Co for the construction of the main block and octagons came to £29,000. Overspending on Government projects is not, it seems, a modern phenomenon.

The Temperate House, backdrop to the fireworks at the annual Summer Swing concerts.

CREATING THE LAKE

The chosen site in the then-new arboretum was raised 2 metres by creating a huge terrace of sand and gravel excavated from, and creating, the lake site. The plants needed good ventilation, so the house was designed in straight lines. The glazing bars were of wood, not iron, for easy repair and to aid heating, and the aesthetics of the day dictated a decorated cornice at the eaves.

STOP-START BUILDING

Work began in 1860. The octagons were completed in 1861, the centre section in 1862 and foundations for the wings were part laid when work was stopped by the Treasury in 1863. Work was not resumed until more than 30 years later, in August 1895. The south wing was finished in 1897, then the contractor became bankrupt, so the north wing was completed by another in 1898.

CONTINUOUS PLANTING

As soon as the octagons were ready, the entire contents of the 'New Zealand House' were transferred to them. This had been the 'Great Stove', built a hundred years earlier, and was demolished as soon as the plants were removed. Its last trace is found near the Princess of Wales Conservatory, in the shape of an iron frame supporting a fine display of wisteria which once draped the building.

Australian plants, tubs of 'unhappy trees' from the Orangery, and some palms from the now-crowded Palm House were all soon established in their new beds. The central interior had 20 oblong beds, with lines of araucarias, palms, tree-ferns and other tall plants in the middle, side beds of rhododendrons, acacias, camellias and magnolias, with smaller plants in pots and boxes on benches. The admiring public were first admitted in May 1863, when the Temperate House was barely two-thirds finished.

THE LATER YEARS

In 1977, a little over a hundred years later, a full restoration was started. The Temperate House is a Grade I listed building, so scrupulous care was taken to keep the integrity of the original design. Just as Burton had used the best materials available to him, so the renovation used the best available - an aluminium and neoprene glazing system - but kept faithful to his design and the rhythm of the original sashes.

Modern heating technology keeps the building frost free - about 6-7°C - over the winter. It uses heat exchangers situated in the basements of the octagons, with intense heat piped from the main boilerhouse a quarter of a mile away.

A NEW LEASE OF LIFE

Some 140 years after work commenced, the Temperate House stands proud as another of Kew's iconic buildings, housing a fascinating and important collection. It also provides a dramatic backdrop to Kew's immensely popular annual summer concerts. Not so well-known is the fact that at night, the building comes magically alive as one of the most spectacular corporate event venues in the world. Totally unique, the Temperate House is perfect for both corporate entertaining and private events. The lush environment is the epitome of the exotic, capable of turning any event into a once-in-a-lifetime experience.

Dinner among the palms

KEW'S MOST COMPLEX GLASSHOUSE, WITH TEN DIFFERENT COMPUTER CONTROLLED ENVIRONMENTS IN ONE BUILDING.

Opened by Diana, Princess of Wales on 28 July 1987, this most complex of Kew's public glasshouses commemorates Princess Augusta who married Frederick, Prince of Wales, in 1736 and who founded the Gardens.

Ten different environments cover the whole range of conditions in the tropics, ranging from scorching arid desert to moist tropical rainforest - all under one roof. Water features strongly in the humid zones, with pools of fish and the famous giant Amazonian waterlily.

Plants of great economic importance are growing here, such as pepper, bananas and pineapples. There are also orchids and carnivorous plants; leaf-cutter ants and impressively large fish in the ponds.

A HUGE ATTRACTION
The giant Amazonian waterlily (*Victoria amazonica*) was a huge attraction in Victorian times. A close relative (*Victoria* 'Longwood hybrid') is just as popular today, with its leaves measuring a full 2 m (6 ft 6 ins) across and flowers that change colour from white to deep pink over 24-36 hours.

FRIEND OR FO
A pitcher plant attracts insects with glistenin droplets of nectar. Once inside, insects lo their footing on the slippery walls and fa into the digestive liquid in the base of t plant. However, the larvae of son other insects have develop immunity to the digesti fluids and thrive on t food remnants th the plant does not us

LIZARDS THAT LUN
Some lizards, including the spi *Acanthosaurus armata*, were confiscate under the CITES agreement (see p 8. and donated to Kew. They are used biological control in the Princess of Wal Conservatory and the Palm House, whe they thrive on a diet of insect pest They are very rarely seen during the da

Conservatory

THE TIME CAPSULE

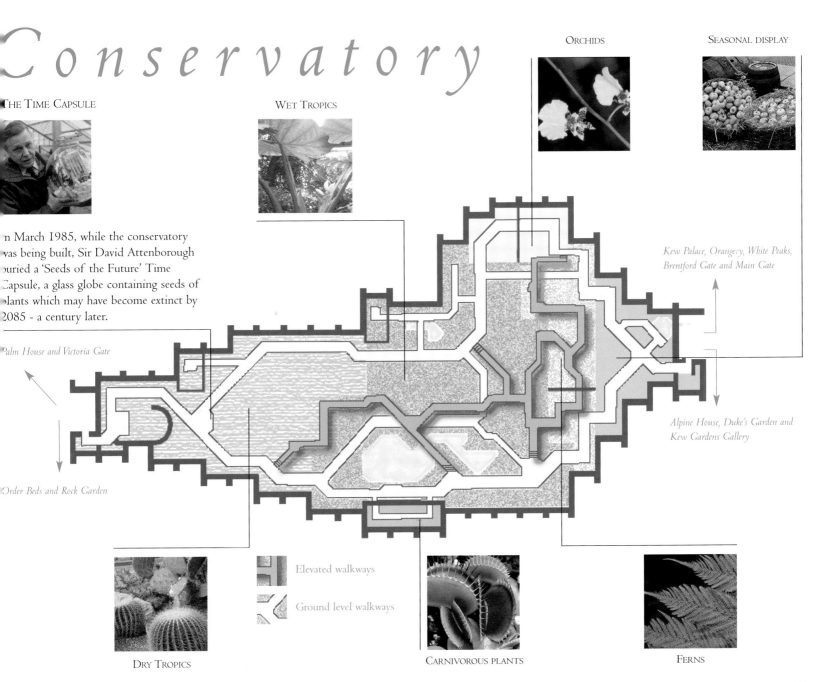

In March 1985, while the conservatory was being built, Sir David Attenborough buried a 'Seeds of the Future' Time Capsule, a glass globe containing seeds of plants which may have become extinct by 2085 - a century later.

WET TROPICS

ORCHIDS

SEASONAL DISPLAY

Kew Palace, Orangery, White Peaks, Brentford Gate and Main Gate

Palm House and Victoria Gate

Alpine House, Duke's Garden and Kew Gardens Gallery

Order Beds and Rock Garden

Elevated walkways

Ground level walkways

DRY TROPICS

CARNIVOROUS PLANTS

FERNS

The Princess of Wales

From wet tropics to arid lands, and a variety in between, explore a whole new world of exotic and economic herbaceous plants

Two main climate zones, the Dry Tropics and Wet Tropics, occupy most of this conservatory. There are eight more different micro-climates in the conservatory, each created for the special needs of a particular plant group. All plants are shown as naturalistically as possible, with ferns clinging to dripping rock faces, and climbers on columns. Paths on different levels bring visitors close to the plants so they can appreciate the subtle details of the vegetation.

THE DRY TROPICS ZONE

This zone represents arid regions from around the world. Here, there are plants that have adopted many different ways of dealing with the lack of water in their environment, conserving it with waxy skins or fleecy jackets, or storing it in succulent stems. Some of the cacti and agaves are displayed against a painted diorama, forming an atmospheric desert backdrop.

Although coming from opposite sides of the world, the agaves and aloes nearby show many similarities in adaptations for survival in these conditions, while the superbly camouflaged 'living stones' can hardly be seen at all until their bright coloured flowers appear.

There are also collections of the unique native plants from the Canary Islands and Madagascar, many of which are threatened as their habitats in the wild are destroyed.

CAMOUFLAGE TECHNIQUES
Plants called 'living stones' (*Lithops*) are so well camouflaged in their surroundings that they are safe from animal grazing - until they flower.

Conservatory

The Seasonally Dry Zone is an enclosure watered sparingly in the winter. It contains plants from the East African savannah, which have all adapted in different ways. For example, the baobab stores water in its thick trunk, while acacias shed leaves in the dry season to conserve water.

Nearly 20% of the world's population lives on the edge of desert, where drought and often inappropriate farming techniques bring danger to semi-arid ecosystems. Kew is learning more from its living collection, studying the use of plants as sustainable crops for food, fuel, fodder and medicine, and to help slow down the rate of desertification.

THE WET TROPICS ZONE

This large area is maintained with the high humidity typical of rainforests. The planting also reflects the lighting conditions; low at floor level where species such as the marantas, with their attractively patterned leaves, are flourishing. Also on show are the wild forms of many familiar house plants, such as the Swiss cheese plant, the African violet and begonias.

SPECIAL AREAS FOR PARTICULAR PLANTS

Even higher humidity, but cool shade, is required for plants from the high cloud forests, so a separate enclosed area is specially set aside for them.

Carnivorous plants are found in cool, well-lit areas and, since they often grow on poor soils, need to supplement their diets by catching insects. The best known species, the Venus flytraps and pitcher plants, are well represented in a section to the east of the Conservatory.

Two distinct zones have been designed to provide the growing conditions that different types of orchids require. A hot, steamy zone features many tropical epiphytic or air-rooting varieties with spectacular showy flowers and specific adaptations to an aerial environment in the rainforest canopy. The cooler orchid zone is more suited to species from the mountainous regions of the tropics - those with their roots in the earth. Many orchids bought rooted in pots from garden centres are in fact epiphytic, and can do well, but at Kew, the conditions in which they live in the wild are replicated as closely as possible.

GOLD, FRANKINCENSE AND MYRRH
Boswellia sacra is the source of frankincense from biblical times - a resin that comes from wounds in the tree which, when dried, had medicinal qualities as a general antiseptic. There is a relative of myrrh at Kew, but sadly, the collection lacks gold.

Ferns, too, come from both tropical and temperate regions and there are two separate areas for ferns which reflect their different needs. The imposing stag's horn ferns, as splendid as the name suggests, are tropical ferns which perch on trees or rocks.

Another popular feature of the Princess of Wales Conservatory are the regularly changed displays at the northern end, showing seasonally themed indoor landscapes.

The Princess of Wales

The design challenge for a major new glasshouse at Kew was both technical and aesthetic. Technically, it had to replace no fewer than 26 elderly glasshouses with one advanced and sophisticated building. Aesthetically, the site was exceptionally sensitive, being close to existing works of the past 'greats' - Burton's Palm House and Chambers' Orangery.

The keynote for the design was the highest possible energy efficiency allied to the lowest possible maintenance costs. It's a simple fact of life that the high humidity and high temperature needed to support life for tropical plants mean a slow death for inappropriate buildings.

With its stepped and angled glass construction, without sidewalls and with most of its space below ground, the

conservatory is a most effective collector of solar energy. The volume is relatively low in relation to its floor area so that temperatures within the individual zones may be altered quickly.

Above all, the Princess of Wales Conservatory looks stunning. The old adage that 'form follows function' is as perfectly demonstrated today as it was over 160 years ago in Burton's day. It looks absolutely in place in its surroundings, even in such imposing company. It is beautifully landscaped, too, blending into the Rock and Woodland Gardens to the east and south and surrounded by the mature trees of the Arboretum to the north and west.

Ten different environments, ranging from the extreme temperatures of desert to the suffocatingly moist heat of mangrove swamps, are controlled by computer to provide different levels of heat, humidity and light.

The technology involved is quite awesome. Sensors on walls and in beds report exact environmental conditions to the computer, which commands heat to flow, ventilation to open, or mists to spray to increase humidity. It is almost as if the building itself is a living organism.

The underground boiler room is a temple to today's technology. Also beneath the conservatory, there are two 227,000 litre (50,000 gallon) storage tanks for rainwater collected from the roof slopes and used, after filtration and ultraviolet treatment, for irrigation and replenishment of the ponds.

Designed for an estimated life of 100 years, it is fascinating to wonder if the Princess of Wales Conservatory will be as compelling in its future old age as Burton's creations are today. Judging from the crowds, the comments and the awards, the omens seem good.

AWARD WINNING DESIGN

Just two awards among many: the Princess of Wales Conservatory was presented with the Institution of Structural Engineers' special award in 1987 and the highly prestigious Europa Nostra Award for Conservation in 1989.

Kew's other plant houses

THE EVOLUTION HOUSE

Stepping out of the Temperate House and walking through 600 million years of plant evolution is a fascinating experience.
The story in the Evolution House begins 4 billion years ago with the lifeless, barren landscape that would have existed until the first true plants - ancestors of modern algae - appeared in the seas some 600 million years ago.

Land plants developed 450 million years ago and the first vascular plants - those with conducting channels or 'veins' for carrying sap - and the ancestors of today's mosses and liverworts, soon evolved.

The Evolution House concentrates on three major periods in plant evolution - the Silurian, Carboniferous and Cretaceous periods - and includes a coal swamp showing the giant clubmosses and horsetails from 300 million years ago. Cycads appeared 200 million years ago followed by conifers and the flowering plants, which dominate the plant kingdom today.

Among the species featured here are the world's largest horsetail (*Equisetum giganteum*) and the high-climbing fern *Lygodium*, whose fronds can grow to over 30 m (97.5 ft) long.

COAL - BLACK MAGIC?

In the Carboniferous period of geological time, clubmosses, tree ferns and giant horsetails flourished in warm damp conditions in extensive areas of wetlands. When these plants died, they fell into the airless morass where, instead of rotting away, they created coal swamps.

Coal is formed when a large concentration of plant debris is buried and subjected to moderately high temperatures and pressures.
For example, geological events such as earthquakes or volcanic activity might bury the plants under many metres of rock or water.
Under these conditions, various chemicals are driven out, the structure becomes fossilised and eventually turns to coal. The process started some 360 million years ago and went through stages, forming first peat and then lignite, or soft brown coal, before hard, black coal was created.

'Steam coal', still used to fire trains and other industrial steam engines in many parts of the world, is one of the coals which sometimes split to reveal well-preserved fossil plants.
The models of giant clubmosses on display here are based on such fossils found in coal.

Model of giant woodlouse (*Arthropleura*) that would have lived at the time of the coal swamps.

Map

↑ Lake and Conservation Area

← Japanese Gateway and Pagoda

→ Palm House and Main Gate

CAVE

CAVE ENTRANCE   ROCK FACE

CRETACEOUS
145-65 million years ago (MYA)

ROCKY OUTCROP

CARBONIFEROUS
360-290 MYA

COAL SWAMP

SILURIAN
435-410 MYA

ROCK BRIDGE

PRECAMBRIAN
More than 570 MYA

EVOLUTION HOUSE
ENTRANCE

TEMPERATE HOUSE

EVOLUTIONARY GROUPS

Just like humans and apes, many plants are related from a common ancestor in prehistory. There are many similarities between senecio and rudbeckia, for example, and their common origins are recognised by placing both in the same Compositae family. Living descendants of some of the examples in the Evolution House are cycads in the Palm House and Temperate House; conifers in the Arboretum; and ferns in the Princess of Wales Conservatory. More family resemblances in the world of flowering plants may be seen in the Order Beds by the Alpine House, and in the neighbouring Grass Garden.

Kew's other plant houses

WATERLILY HOUSE & ALPINE HOUSE

REPRODUCTION WITH BED AND BREAKFAST INCLUDED

When working in the Amazon forests, one of Kew's previous directors, Sir Ghillean Prance, discovered how giant waterlilies are pollinated. The flowers open at dusk, when their scent attracts beetles, who spend all night feeding on nectar as the flower closes around them. The next evening, when the flower reopens, the beetles - now covered in pollen - move on to another bloom, pollinating it in return for their 'bed and breakfast'.

THE WATERLILY HOUSE

Just by the Palm House, this is another of Kew's classic listed buildings, again with ironwork by Richard Turner. Built in 1852, it was then the widest single span glasshouse in the world, designed specifically to house the huge attraction of the age, the giant Amazonian waterlily.

Sadly, the huge plant never did well and in 1866, the house was converted into an Economic Plant House for medicinal and culinary plants. However, in 1991, it was converted back to its original use and today, it is the hottest and most humid environment at Kew and contains, as well as waterlilies, other very interesting plants.

In summer, the *Nymphaea* waterlilies and a giant *Victoria cruziana* put on a beautifully serene display. Sacred lotus and papyrus both thrive in these hot, humid conditions. In the corner beds, there are plants of economic importance such as rice, taro, bananas, manioc, sugar cane and lemon grass. High up, there are some spectacular gourds - fruits of some members of the cucumber family, such as loofahs and hedgehog and wax gourds. The Waterlily House is closed in winter.

Lake, Bamboo Garden and Rhododendron Dell

Lilac Garden, Whit and Brentfo

WATERLILY HO

Princess of Wales Conserva

44

THE ALPINE HOUSE

This is the smallest of Kew's glasshouses, yet it offers a very wide range of different species of plants, with displays generally changing twice a week. Alpines spend their winter dry and dormant, protected by a thick insulating layer of snow. Melting snow gives them moisture for growth, beginning a short growing season, with intense light during spring and a relatively cool, dry summer.

This is the third Alpine House at Kew and its high-tech construction and systems are designed to control temperature, moisture and light levels and air flow to replicate alpine habitats accurately. There is even a refrigerated bench in the centre to aid the cultivation of plants from arctic and equatorial mountain conditions. The size of the house is in keeping with the smallness of the plants and the pyramid shape reflects mountain landscapes. The moat surrounding the house not only collects rainwater to feed the pond inside, but also moisturises and cools the air drawn into the house through special louvres, so helping to create a truly alpine atmosphere.

WINTER PROTECTION

Some plants survive the cold by insulating themselves with dense, fur-like hairs. Others trap daytime heat in their swollen stems and conserve it for freezing nights. Giant lobelias (*Lobelia keniensis* - left) on Mount Kenya grow taller than humans and have not only hairs, but a 'lagging' of dead leaves around their stems. Some alpines and plants from the frozen earth regions called the tundra, protect themselves against strong winds by adopting a ground-hugging posture. The saxifrages are good examples - *Saxifraga cochlearis* also has small overlapping leaves to conserve moisture and a white waxy secretion to reflect strong sunlight.

SUNBURN FOR ALPINES?
In strong bright sunlight in high clear mountain air, humans are very susceptible to sunburn. It's exactly the same for plants and the red pigment on some alpines protects them against the effects of UV radiation and helps to absorb heat. The energy gained by these plants, like the *Sempervivum tectorum*, keeps them up to 12°C warmer than air temperature.

Orangery, White Peaks and Main Gate

Palm House and Victoria Gate

ALPINE HOUSE

Kew's special gardens an

DUKE'S GARDEN · GRASS GARDEN · AQUATIC GARDEN · SECLUDED GARDEN

One of Kew's greatest charms is the sense of discovery. Turn a corner, follow a different path, and there's a stunning garden, or themed planting, showing not just the beauty of the plants but the relationships between them, often realised for the first time. New knowledge and deeper understanding are great joys, too - and very much a part of the pleasure of Kew.

DUKE'S GARDEN

The walled Duke's Garden is planted more for pleasure than science. Familiar shrubs and herbaceous perennials around large lawns give floral interest throughout the year. The *Duchess Border*, along the outside of one of the walls, is home to the Lavender Species Collection, with both well-known garden lavenders and a number of tender species, rarely grown in the UK. Various Mediterranean specimens are trialled here to determine their hardiness in the south of England.

The *Gravel Garden*, sponsored by Thames Water, shows a wide range of attractive plants needing less water than traditional English garden choices. This tranquil walled area is also an ideal, sheltered spot for the *Half-hardy Herbaceous Garden*, with its attractive display of more tender plants, prized by gardeners, but rather restricted as to where they can be grown.

GRASS
GARDEN

AQUATIC
GARDEN

DUKE'S
GARDEN

GRASS GARDEN

Designed in 1982, the Grass Garden contai 550 species and the count is rising. Grasse (Gramineae, also known as Poaceae) are some of the most economically important plants, supplying food directly as cereals a indirectly as cattle fodder; they are the bas of many alcoholic drinks; and are used in building - straw thatch and bamboo - whi sorghum and sugar cane (grown in the Waterlily House and Palm House) are use to produce petrol substitutes.

Visit in early summer for temperate annua grasses and cereals, and autumn for the perennials and their seed heads. Other display beds have British native grasses, tropical and temperate cereals, and specim lawns showing different mixes of grass seed for different purposes. Of all the ornamentals, *Miscanthus sinensis* is notable for both its history - now a widely used architectural plant but having been grown from a single batch of seed - and its futur being investigated at Kew as an alternative and renewable fuel source.

hemed plantings

AQUATIC GARDEN

Best visited in the height of summer when the waterlilies and aquatic plants are in full flower, the Aquatic Garden was opened in 1909, complete with hot water pipes to give the plants an early start. Today, some 40 varieties of waterlilies and more than 70 other plants such as sedges and rushes, are grown in containers in the central and corner tanks at ambient water temperatures, while the long side tanks hold floating aquatics. As well as the beautiful waterlilies, the flowering rush and the bog bean are fine specimens.

SECLUDED GARDEN

This relaxed and intimate cottage-style garden is designed to appeal to all the senses, illustrated with poems on sight, scent, hearing and touch. Behind earth mounds, pleached limes form a hedge on tall stems to circle a spiral fountain. A stream is bordered with waterside plantings and scented flowers.

Even bad days are interesting when rain splashes off the giant leaves of *Gunnera tinctoria* and wind rustles through a tunnel of whispering bamboos. The plants here most closely resemble private gardens, with apple, pear and quince trees, roses, pelargoniums, lilies, irises and cistus.

SECLUDED
GARDEN

> *"I am at Kew, profiting by the exceptional summer to throw myself into 'plein air' studies in this wonderful garden of Kew. Oh! My dear friend, what trees! what lawns! what undulations of the ground!"*
>
> Camille Pissarro, visiting London, 1892

Some of the 'undulations of the ground' that so delighted Pissarro may well have started with something as prosaic as a gravel pit. Some 'ups and downs' are perfectly matched - the mound on which the Temperate House stands is spoil dug excavating the Lake. One thing is certain, however, that his delight with the Gardens, so enthusiastically expressed more than a century ago, is an experience shared by Kew's visitors today.

WOODLAND GARDEN
ROCK GARDEN
ORDER BEDS
ROSE PERGOLA

WOODLAND GARDEN

Here, a charming garden exactly replicates nature's design, since it is in three layers. High up, a deciduous tree canopy of oaks and birches supports climbers and shades the middle layer of deciduous shrubs such as maples and rhododendrons which, in their turn, protect the ground-cover layer, including hellebores, primulas, Himalayan blue poppies and North American trilliums.

HELLEBORES AND PEONIES are tough hardy herbaceous and shrubby perennials. Visitors envious of the splendid hellebores should be reminded of the secret for success, which is never to disturb the roots. A few years ago, a panellist on BBC Radio 4's *Gardeners' Question Time* told the story of how his mother moved her much-loved 'Christmas Rose'. He told her that moving it was the last thing ever to do to a hellebore. So she moved it back again! Scientists at Kew are currently working on the correct classification of peonies (*Paeonia*).

Rock Garden

The first rock garden was designed in 1882 to look like a Pyrennean mountain valley. It is now built from sandstone, which retains more water than the original limestone, and has been redesigned to include a central bog garden and cascade. This makes for a wider variety of environments, in which alpines, Mediterranean plants and woodland and moisture-loving plants flourish. The alpines have a well-drained soil and a grit mulch to prevent water splashing on to their leaves; Mediterranean plants (from five regions of the world with similar climates) are in the sunniest spots, again with well-drained soil; while the woodland plants enjoy the shade and damp conditions created by the water features.

There are six global regions represented in Kew's attractive Rock Garden. Visitors used to domestic rock gardens are intrigued both by the size of the display and being able to walk through it, by the waterfalls and gullies; and by the truly extraordinary variety of the world's plants on show here.

Order Beds

The Order Beds are a 'living library' of flowering plants for students of botany and horticulture, as they are arranged systematically in family groups, so they can be easily located for study. The grouping of plants, and the science of understanding the relationship between them, is called *taxonomy* and there is more information on this in 'What's in a name?' on pages 76 & 77. Science apart, the Order Beds are stunning to see in full summer bloom.

Rose Pergola

A pergola covered with a variety of climbing roses is a deservedly popular feature in the central path of the Order Beds, while the surrounding walls support many fine climbing plants, such as *Actinidia kolomikta* with its striking pink, red and white spring foliage.

49

"I never had any other Desire so Strong and so like to Covetousness, as that one which I have had alwa[ys] that I might be Master at last of a small House and large Garden ... and there to dedicate the Remain[s] of my Life to the Culture of them, and study of nature."

Abraham Cowley (1618-67) English poet and essayist

The gardens on these pages are in the general area of the original Botanic Garden started by Princess Augusta. Three of Kew's notable trees are here; the maidenhair tree, the nearby North American locust tree, and the gnarled Japanese pagoda tree, all of which are reliably believed to date from the 1760s. There's a fine mulberry - but no silkworms - and a glorious wisteria on the site of William Chambers' Great Stove. The elegant Broad Walk is a prominent feature (see p 56).

QUEEN'S GARDEN & BEE GARDEN

WINTER GARDEN

ICE HOUSE

QUEEN'S GARDEN

Kew Palace is the oldest building at Kew (see p70) and behind it, there is a charming 17th century style garden. The word 'style' is used advisedly because despite its historically impeccable appearance, it was conceived in 1959 by Sir George Taylor, then Director of the Royal Botanic Gardens, and officially opened by H.M. Queen Elizabeth II ten years later.

One element is a parterre enclosed in box hedges and planted with lavender, sage, cotton lavender and rosemary. Standing in the pond in the centre of the parterre is a copy of Verocchio's 'Boy with a Dolphin', the original of which is in Florence's Palazzo Vecchio.

The plants in the Queen's Garden are exclusively those grown in Britain before and during the 17th century. Their labelling differs from Kew's norm, since they include not only today's botanical name and family, but also:-

the common name in the 17th century

a virtue, or quotation from a herbal (plant book) and

the author's name and date of publication.

There is a great deal to see in the Queen's Garden a wrought iron pillar from Hampton Court Palace, a chamomile chair, intricately plaited laburnums forming an arch, pleached hornbeams, a mound covered in clipped box, with a gazebo and a fine smoke tree.

BEE GARDEN

No English garden is complete without its bees and Kew is no exception. Developed in 1993, the Bee Garden has three styles of beehive, from simple logs and basketware skeps, to modern wooden hives that grow taller as more 'supers' (extra layers) are inserted as the honeycombs form inside them. Two colonies had new queens flown in from New Zealand where bees are traditionally quite docile. The Bee Garden is full of flowers popular with the bees and shows the important interaction between plants and insects. Without the pollinators, plants would not set seed and our food supplies would dwindle rapidly.

WINTER GARDEN

The Winter Garden around the Ice House (see p 67) is laid out for real interest on grey days. Both sight and scent come into play in this aesthetically satisfying garden, where specimens are set off against an evergreen backdrop, perfect for those which flower on bare wood. Here, *Mahonia* x *media* 'Winter Sun', winter box and the chocolate-scented *Azara microphylla* surround wintersweets, viburnums, flowering quince, cornelian cherries, witch hazel and willows with their yellow catkins. There are bulbs, too, planted under the woody specimens, with winter aconite, snowdrops and windflowers left to naturalise. Conservationists will note *Abeliophyllum distichum* which is endangered in its native Korea.

"Go to Kew in lilac-time ... and you shall wander hand in hand with love in summer's wonderland."
From 'The Barrel-Organ' by Alfred Noyes (1880-1958)

LILAC GARDEN

The poet Alfred Noyes was enchanted by lilacs at Kew and rightly so, as they are among the most elegant and colourful of all early-flowering shrubs. Several lilacs, including the Chinese species *Syringa julianae* and *Syringa sweginzowii*, came into cultivation through Kew's lilac collection. Today's Lilac Garden is the result of a replanting completed in 1997. Most lilacs are cultivated from eastern Europe's *Syringa vulgaris*, but lilacs can also be found through the Himalayas to the mountains of China where the greatest diversity occurs.

In Kew's Lilac Garden, best viewed in early June, there are 105 specimens in ten beds arranged according to their cultivation and breeding history. As well as the *Syringa* species, there are 'Chinese' lilacs based on the hybrid *Syringa x chinensis*, developed in Rouen, France, with a rounded habit and paired flower spikes, and 'Hyacinthiflora' hybrids from a cross between *Syringa vulgaris* and the early flowering Chinese species *Syringa oblata*. The late flowering Villosae lilacs bred in Canada by Isabella Preston and the Pubescente cultivars, with their hairy leaves and relatively small size, also put on excellent shows.

ROSE GARDEN

This is a major focus for visitors, near the Palm House and in full glorious bloom from June to August. Cluster-flowered and large-flowered rose are arranged by colour; red nearer the Palm House, contrasting against the white building; shading out to lighter colours at the perimeter, where white and yellow roses are set against the green hedges and vistas.

Each of the 54 beds contains a different cultivar of rose, all available through British rose growers. Ten of the beds illustrate the hybridisation of roses through the centuries.

The semicircular holly hedge and sunken areas a historically important, being the remains of an 1845 design by William Nesfield, which include the Broad Walk and the three great vistas.

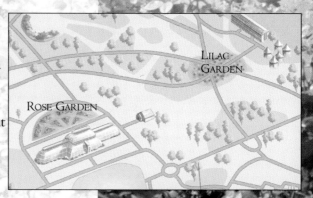

ROSE GARDEN

LILAC GARDEN

RHODODENDRON DELL

Another of Kew's famed single plantings is the rhododendrons - one of the largest and showiest groups of flowering shrubs, with great variation in size, habit and form. There are over 700 specimens planted in the Dell, with some unique hybrids found only here. This is not a natural valley, but a creation of 'Capability' Brown, who carved what he called the 'Hollow Walk' out of the Thames flood plain in 1773.

In the 1850s, Sir Joseph Hooker started his spectacular rhododendron collection with specimens gathered on his Himalayan expeditions. The oldest specimen is *Rhododendron campanulatum*; the most highly scented are *Rhododendron kewense* 'King George' and *Rhododendron loderi*. Flowering continues from November to August, with most at their best in late May. The brilliant mass of white flowers each spring comes from the largest planting, 'Cunningham's White', which thrives in the local conditions, shaded by trees and kept humid by the Thames nearby.

AZALEA GARDEN

Anyone looking for azaleas to grow for their blaze of late spring colour will be spoilt for choice at Kew. Twelve different groups of azalea hybrids have appeared since the very first Ghent hybrids in the 1820s and the garden's two circles of beds arrange the plants in date order, leading up to today's varieties from eastern America and Holland. All the species planted in the Azalea Walk leading into the garden belong to a group of deciduous azaleas from North America and Japan. Those in the two beds nearest the Azalea Garden have been used for breeding.

MAGNOLIA COLLECTION

The first exotic magnolia was introduced to this country in the seventeenth century. Many of these deciduous and evergreen shrubs and trees with their spectacular pink, cream or white flowers, do very well here, as can be seen from April to June in a superb planting near the rhododendrons and azaleas.

BAMBOO GARDEN

Any time is a good time to visit the Bamboo Garden where the design makes the most of the variety of forms, stem colours and leaf shapes. The contrast given by the Chusan palms is particularly striking.

Bamboos are woody grasses ranging in form from giant poles, through wispy variegated species, to fountains of leaves from the pendulous varieties. Some hardy in the UK can reach 3 m (10 ft) high, others can be mown as lawns! Bamboos grow wild on every continent except Europe and people use them for everything from food to building materials. Look out for the Chinese walking stick bamboo with its knobbly stems.

Some species can be highly invasive, so strong barriers are used to contain them. Kew's bamboos are scientifically studied for classification and growth patterns.

The Arboretum

"This great society is going smash;
They cannot fool us with how fast they go,
How much they cost each other and the gods!
A culture is no better than its woods."

W H Auden *Shield of Achilles* (1955) 'Bucolics'

What is it about woodlands and trees? Mankind's fascination with them must be rooted in prehistory, when they provided shelter and fuel, weapons and tools. Exotic trees have been collected at Kew since its earliest days, but it was during the stewardship of Sir Joseph Hooker (the son of Kew's first Director, Sir William Hooker) that today's Arboretum took shape.

WOODLAND GLADE

The Woodland Glade is notable for its giant redwoods and other majestic conifers, underplanted with shrubs for summer and late autumn colour. There's a sense of great calm by the charming Waterlily Pond with its profusion of aquatic life as well as the plants.

BERBERIS DELL

Created between 1869 and 1875, this was once a gravel pit and is Kew's third-biggest excavation after the Lake and Rhododendron Dell. Its rather secluded character and large collection of berberis and mahonias make it well worth a visit. Most of the berberis family are fully hardy in Britain and grow well in most soils. Flowers in shades of yellow and orange bloom from early spring to late summer, while the autumn fruit can be red, black or blue.

HIGHLY COLOURED

Autumn colour reaches its peak with the vibrant leaves of the maples between the Temperate House and the Flagpole; while still more colour comes from the berries and foliage on various trees of the Rosaceae (rose) family; whitebeams, rowans, hawthorns and crab apples.

CHERRY WALK

Stretching from the Rose Garden behind the Palm House to the Temperate House, Cherry Walk is a superb collection of Japanese ornamental cherry trees. Replanting the original 1935 walk was completed in 1996 and now, 22 trees in 11 matched pairs of different cultivars make a spectacular show in spring. The charming and expressive Japanese names for the cherries include *Imose* (sweetheart), *Tai Haku* (big white flowers) and *Taki-nioi* (fragrant waterfall).

THE LAKE

There have always been water features at Kew and this lake, which despite appearances, is artificial, was started with the present Pinetum and extended when the Temperate House was built. Moisture-loving trees and shrubs are planted all round and there are ornamental waterfowl (see p 60) on the water and the surrounding lawns.

HOLLY WALK

Holly Walk is an important historical feature, planted along what used to be Love Lane on the main public right of way from Kew to Richmond.

It was originally laid out in 1874 by Sir Joseph Hooker as part of a series of vistas. Most of the hollies are original - over 135 years old - and many are now large trees. The walk remains the way it was intended through propagation of the original specimens

At over 1030 m (3390 ft) in length, Holly Walk is the largest, most comprehensive collection of mature hollies in cultivation. They typically flower in June in a mass of white flowers and the berries, which vary from red to black or white depending on the species, are at their best in November and December, but continue through to the spring.

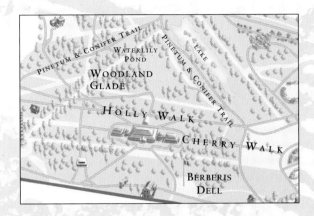

THE PINETUM AND CONIFER TRAIL

The first Pinetum at Kew was planted over 200 years ago - 36 trees in the original botanic garden. The second was on land donated by Queen Victoria and some of those conifers remain by the Waterlily House. Today's Pinetum was started in 1870 by Sir Joseph Hooker, when the trees were laid out with related species grouped together.

The Conifer Trail consists of 19 clearly labelled trees, representing eight of the nine conifer families and showing the enormous diversity within the group. The ninth family, the Phyllocladaceae, is tropical and cannot be grown in the open here. The Conifer Trail leaflet describes the trees, their origins and uses in detail; and following it is a delight.

The Broad Walk and

SIR WILLIAM HOOKER, DECIMUS BURTON AND WILLIAM NESFIELD:
THE 19TH CENTURY VISIONARIES WHO SHAPED TODAY'S KEW GARDENS

The development of Kew Gardens can be divided into two main periods, before and after 1845, when the gardens expanded to some 110 hectares (274 acres). It was then that the vision of Sir William Hooker, the first full-time Director; Decimus Burton, the supervising architect; and William Nesfield, the principal landscape designer, shaped the grand glasshouses and great sweeps of planting and landscaping so familiar and so admired today.

It was not always harmonious. Nesfield and Hooker had differences where design confronted taxonomy. Nesfield's creativity was stifled, he felt, by Hooker's insistence on grouping trees by their botanical relationships, not by size, colour and form. Hooker, on his part, said that highly ornamental parterres were not consistent with the nature of the Arboretum. However, the gaining of more land satisfied their needs.

By autumn 1845, Nesfield's plan for the entire gardens included the Broad Walk, lined with deodar cedars interspersed with flower beds; the Pond to the east of the Palm House, which had new parterres either side of it; the Pinetum and enlarged Arboretum; and new walks, vistas and paths

The vistas and avenues are Nesfield's indelible signature on today's Kew.
In a 'goose foot' pattern radiating from the Palm House, Syon Vista was a wide gravel-laid walk stretching 1,200 m (3,937 ft) towards the Thames; Pagoda Vista was a handsome grassed walk some 850 m (2,800 ft) long; while the third, short, vista fanned from the northwest corner of the Palm House and focused on a single cedar of Lebanon towards Kew Palace.

These vistas and the parterres demonstrated the importance of Burton's Palm House to Kew and although many of the original formal beds have long since vanished, the impact of the grand plan remains to this day

three great vistas

RESTORING NESFIELD'S BROAD WALK

Kew has embarked upon a plan to restore the grandeur of Nesfield's original planting design on the once-majestic Broad Walk. Sixteen semi-mature Atlantic cedars now take the place of Nesfield's deodar cedars. The Atlantic cedar looks very similar to the deodar, but grows better in London. They will eventually be joined by summer-planted oak containers near the pathway itself.

Moving plants can be tricky. Moving trees needs even more care and enormous power. An excellent tree transplanter, capable of carrying trees up to 20 m (66 ft) in height, had been designed by William Barron. Kew bought one in 1866 and used it to great effect, one winter transplanting 60 trees weighing up to seven tonnes each.

To move a tree, a deep trench had to be dug 2 m (6 ft 6 ins) away from, and all round the trunk. The transplanter's side beams were removed and the machine reassembled round the tree. A cradle was placed under the root ball and a system of ropes, pulleys and winches heaved the tree, upright, out of the ground. A team of horses then dragged the entire contraption to a prepared hole for replanting.

A fully restored Barron's Tree Transplanter being used to mark the start of the Broad Walk restoration in early November 2000.

Wildlife and conservation

That Kew is a world class botanic garden, there is no doubt. However, among its millions of visitors, less is known about Kew's global reputation as a centre of excellence for plant research. Kew scientists undertake the basic plant identification and classification studies that underpin all other scientific and conservation activities related to those plants.

There is also an enormous amount of scientific effort put into supporting conservation and sustainable use of plant resources in the UK and overseas (see pp 82-87). To underline Kew's conservation activity, the Millennium Seed Bank at Wakehurst Place is the most comprehensive seed conservation project in the world (see pp 92-93).

Conservation and wildlife go hand in hand. Conservation of habitat is vital for the survival of plant species and for the wildlife that depends upon them. The interdependence of the plant and animal kingdoms is a fascinating study, at its most basic being insects and other animals relying on plants for food, while plants need the animals' help in pollination, and then dispersal of the seeds produced. A simple case of mutual survival. Without the care and conservation of plants, mankind will die too.

COMPOST - HEAPS OF INTEREST

Peat - for years, every gardener's first choice for potting and seed composts - is a rapidly dwindling natural resource and wildlife habitat. Kew suspended the use of peat in 1989, even though peat replacement technology was then in its infancy.

Today, both Kew Gardens and Wakehurst Place have extensive composting programmes and at Kew, there is a viewing platform in the Pinetum, close to the Lake. Kew makes 10,000 cu m of waste plant material every year. This is mixed with horse manure and, after watering and turning through a 10-12 week cycle, 2,000 cu m of compost are produced for use throughout the Gardens.

Rather than using peat, well rotted farmyard or stable manure is an excellent soil conditioner and fertiliser; and mushroom compost is a good substitute. Peat-free soil improvers and potting composts are readily available, while bark chippings and coconut products make good mulches. Recycling garden debris and organic kitchen waste in domestic compost-makers is an excellent plan, not only good for the garden, but relieving pressure on landfill sites.

at Kew

CONSERVATION AREA

There is an extraordinary variety of wildlife at Kew. The Conservation Area in the 15 hectares (37 acres) behind Queen Charlotte's Cottage is managed as a habitat for native flora and fauna. Here, in the heart of southwest London, is a superb bluebell wood kept flourishing by traditional methods such as hazel coppicing, with associated meadow and pond habitats.

The woodland contains native oaks; some elderly exotics such as monkey-puzzle and Turkey oak; and some very rare native trees, such as the Plymouth pear. This small and spiny tree, with marble-sized fruits, is one of Britain's rarest, found in the wild at just a few sites around Plymouth, Devon and in Cornwall. Its survival is guaranteed at Kew and at Wakehurst Place. So, too, is that of the Bristol mountain ash, with only 100 wild trees remaining in the Avon Gorge.

Dead wood is left standing: holes and crevices in trunks make excellent nesting places for birds and bats. It is also left where it falls, as a valuable habitat for insects and other small creatures, which provide food for the birds. Fungi eventually break dead wood down into valuable nutrients for the soil.

A grassy area is kept as it always has been, an uncultivated hay meadow, cut once a year when the grass seeds have set. There are ten grasses - five of which grow nowhere else at Kew - and many wild flowers, which attract thousands of butterflies and other insects in summer.

Larch Pond is an artificial, clay-lined water feature, dug in 1973-4 to provide a balance between open water and vegetation cover. Water plants include reed mace and great water dock, but the most interesting development was the 1993 introduction of 100 great crested newts as part of a national programme to breed, then reintroduce them to safe areas. Changes in farming and new building have meant the loss of many habitats for this rare native newt and Kew is pleased to be part of its re-establishment programme.

Please note that in order to protect many plants - especially the bluebells - from trampling and to keep the Conservation Area as natural and undisturbed as possible, opening is sometimes restricted during particularly sensitive periods, and visitors are asked to keep strictly to the hard-surfaced paths.

Release of great crested newts

Walk on the wild side

WHEN WALKING THROUGH KEW GARDENS, IT IS VERY REWARDING TO LOOK AT MORE THAN THE PLANTS AND THE BUILDINGS. IN THE SKY, ON THE GROUND, IN AND UNDER THE WATER, THERE'S AN ABUNDANCE OF WILDLIFE.

TUFTED DUCK

SHOVELLER

WIDGEON
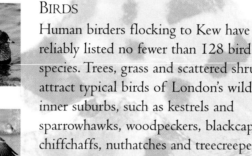

MANDARIN DUCK

POCHARD

CORMORANT
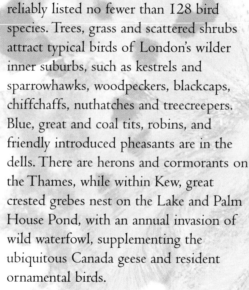

BARNACLE GOOSE

GREYLAG GOOSE

BAR-HEADED GOOSE

EGYPTIAN GOOSE

GREAT CRESTED GREBE

PHEASANT

RING-NECKED PARAKEET
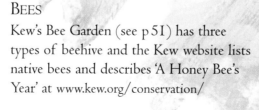

SHELDUCK

BIRDS

Human birders flocking to Kew have reliably listed no fewer than 128 bird species. Trees, grass and scattered shrubs attract typical birds of London's wilder inner suburbs, such as kestrels and sparrowhawks, woodpeckers, blackcaps, chiffchaffs, nuthatches and treecreepers. Blue, great and coal tits, robins, and friendly introduced pheasants are in the dells. There are herons and cormorants on the Thames, while within Kew, great crested grebes nest on the Lake and Palm House Pond, with an annual invasion of wild waterfowl, supplementing the ubiquitous Canada geese and resident ornamental birds.

BEES

Kew's Bee Garden (see p 51) has three types of beehive and the Kew website lists native bees and describes 'A Honey Bee's Year' at www.kew.org/conservation/

BUTTERFLIES

Lepidopterists like Kew. At least 23 species of butterfly belonging to five families have been recorded at Kew since 1980 - a high number considering the London location, but a reflection of the variety of plant life and habitats within the Gardens. Nectar plants are important for the butterflies, but food plants for their caterpillars are just as vital, together with proper habitat management to allow each species to complete its annual life cycle. The mowing regime of many areas at Kew is designed specifically to provide nectar for the adults and sufficient food to see the caterpillars through to their pupal forms. Kew's butterflies are present at some stage of their life in winter, too. Some hibernate as adults, others as caterpillars or pupae, while the remainder overwinter only as eggs. In summer, they are all out, dividing their time between eating and trying to produce the next generation. More information and a table of butterflies at Kew is on the website.

Common Darter

Banded Demoiselle

DRAGONS AND DAMSELS

The difference between a dragonfly and a damselfly is easy to see when they're at rest. Dragonflies keep their wings outstretched like small helicopters, while damselflies fold theirs back along the length of their bodies. Dragonflies are also usually more sturdily

Small Copper

made than slender damselflies. The flying stage for each is only the very last part of their lives, concerned with reproduction, when pairs often fly in tandem, joined at their tails. Water is vital for early life, with eggs sometimes attached to plants under water, or simply dropped into it. When they hatch, it is the larval, or nymph, stage which lasts longest. Nymphs are carnivorous and have fierce prey-seizing jaws on an extendible 'mask', a feature unique to the Odonta family of dragonflies and damselflies. Blue-tailed damselflies are seen from early June around the Lake, with the Common Blue at the Waterlily Pond from July. The dragonflies start flying in July with Brown and Migrant Hawkers and the Common Darter. Hawkers, Darters, Chasers, Skimmers - dragonflies and their close damselfly relatives are a fascinating study - for more extensive information see the Kew website.

FUNGI

Autumn is an especially 'fruitful' time for fungi. What appears above the ground, or from tree trunks and rotting vegetation as mushrooms, toadstools and brackets, is only the fruiting stage, and short-lived at that. The main body of a fungus lives within its source of food, which could be wood or other plant material, the soil, or carrion. Fungi are a separate group, neither plant nor animal, consisting of microscopic threads that form a network that expands out through, and feeds on, organic matter. Fungi are usually the primary decomposers in their habitats, releasing nutrients to the surroundings. About 80% of all plants grow in mutual association with fungi and many, from orchids to pine trees, will not grow without a partner fungus within their root systems - a mycorrhizal association. Scientists at Kew are studying fungi from around the world, investigating their practical uses as biological controls against pests such as insects and eelworms, with the objective of reducing the use of toxic pesticides. There is far more to 'mushrooms' than meets the eye and an illustrated leaflet is normally available at the Victoria Gate Centre in autumn.

The Pagoda

ONE OF KEW'S FAMOUS FEATURES, THE PAGODA IS ONE OF 25 ORNAMENTAL BUILDINGS DESIGNED FOR KEW BY SIR WILLIAM CHAMBERS.

There was a fashion for Chinoiserie in English garden design in the mid 18th century, and Chambers was a keen advocate, using decorative buildings and intricate pathways as a reaction to the sweeping 'natural' lines of contemporaries such as 'Capability' Brown.

The Pagoda was completed in 1762 and was not universally popular. The great man of letters, Sir Horace Walpole, was decidedly sniffy about its construction. Having seen it from Twickenham, where he lived, he complained to a friend that, "In a fortnight you will be able to see it in Yorkshire."

The ten-storey octagonal structure is 163 ft (nearly 50 m) high and was, at that time, the most accurate reconstruction of a Chinese building in Europe (although purists argue that pagodas should always have an odd number of floors). It tapers, with successive floors from the first to the topmost being 1 ft (30 cm) less in diameter and height than the preceding one.

PAYING OFF THE KING'S DEBTS

The original building was very colourful; the roofs being covered with varnished iron plates, with a dragon on each edge. There were 80 dragons in all, each covered in coloured glass. The iron plates were later replaced by slate and the dragons vanished, reportedly sold to pay off some of George IV's debts, according to Joseph Hooker, a Director of Kew, many years later.

In 1843, Decimus Burton wanted to restore the Pagoda to its former glory, but the cost then of £4,350 was considered too high a price to pay.

BOMBS AWAY!

Contemporaries of Chambers often wondered if such a tall building would remain standing, though it had been "buil of very hard bricks". Its sturdy construction was proved in World War II when it survived a close call from a stick o German bombs exploding nearby. This wa ironic, since at the time, holes had been made in each of its floors so that British bomb designers could drop models of their latest inventions from top to bottom to study their behaviour in flight.

RESTORATIONS

There have been several restorations, mainly to the roofs, but the original colours and the dragons have not been replaced, though the question of replica dragons was discussed in 1979. In his comprehensive 'History of the Royal Botanic Gardens, Kew', Ray Desmond describes the Pagoda as "... an uneasy exclamation mark terminating W A Nesfield's vista. The Pagoda still awaits the restoration it richly deserves."

Sir William Chambers (d. 1796)

Born to Scottish parents in Gothenburg in either 1723 or 1726 (references differ), William Chambers went to live in China as an employee of the Swedish East India Company, a stay which sparked his interest in Chinese architecture. At the age of 26, he studied to become an architect and trained classically in Rome. In 1757 he became Princess Augusta's official architect and architectural tutor to her son, the future George III. He supervised the buildings at Augusta's five establishments and, over a five year period, designed 25 decorative buildings for Kew. Many, such as the Mosque, the Alhambra, the Palladian Bridge and Menagerie have disappeared, but the Orangery, the Ruined Arch, the Temple of Bellona and, above all, the Pagoda, are permanent reminders of his talents. His most solid achievement is Somerset House in London, recently restored to its original splendour. He was knighted in 1771 by King Gustav III of Sweden for a series of drawings of Kew Gardens, and George III allowed him to use the title in England.

Even Sparrows
Freed from all fear of man
England in Spring

Kew's Chokushi-Mon (the Gateway of the Imperial Messenger) is a four-fifths size replica of the Karamon of Nishi Hongan-ji in Kyoto, the ancient imperial capital of Japan. The replica was originally built for the Japan-British Exhibition, held in London in 1910, after which it was dismantled and rebuilt in Kew Gardens.

It is the finest example of a traditional Japanese building in Europe, built in the architectural style of the Momoyama (or Japanese rococo) period in the late 16th century, a time of peace, prosperity and flowering creativity.

Typically expressive, Chokushi-Mon shows finely carved woodwork depicting flowers and animals, with the most intricate panels portraying an ancient Chinese legend about the devotion of a pupil to his master.

THE HAIKU

A haiku is a traditional Japanese form of poetry, consisting of exactly seventeen characters or 'beats', always divided into lines of five, seven, five. The best haikus illustrate a truthful moment with penetration, wit, and a *kigo*, or reference to the seasons.

Landscape

Restorations

The Japanese wood-carver, Kumajiro Torii, carried out some detailed repair work in 1936 and 1957, but by 1988, the edifice was badly dilapidated. With generous support from Japan and elsewhere, a full restoration, combining traditional Japanese skills and modern techniques, was completed after a year's painstaking work in November 1995.

Today, Chokushi-Mon is seen in rather more than its original splendour, because as part of the restoration, the original lead-covered cedar-bark roof shingles were replaced with traditional, more dramatic, copper tiles.

The Japanese landscape

Around the Chokushi-Mon, the Japanese landscape is in three distinct areas, each depicting one of the many different aspects of Japanese gardens. Overall, it is a dry stone *kaiyu shiki* (stroll-around) garden in the Momoyama style.

The main entrance leads into a 'Garden of Peace', reminiscent of a tea garden (*roji*), a calming, tranquil place with stone baths and a gently dripping water basin. The slope to the south of Chokushi-Mon is a 'Garden of Activity', symbolising the natural grandeur of waterfalls, hills and the sea. The third area, the 'Garden of Harmony', links the other two and represents the mountainous regions of Japan, using precisely positioned stones and rock outcrops, interplanted with a wide variety of plants of Japanese origin, many of which are well known in the West.

Bamboos

Japanese gardens frequently use bamboos, not just for their graceful shapes, but also for their gentle susurrations as breezes whisper through delicate foliage. In this landscape, the bamboo family is represented by a dwarf fern-leaf variety, *Arundinaria pygmaea* var. *disticha.*

Bamboos are central to Japanese life and culture. Their woody stems are used for workaday construction and fencing, as well as the most delicate of craft and ceremonial objects, such as fans and flutes and the exquisite whisks and dippers used in the tea ceremony.

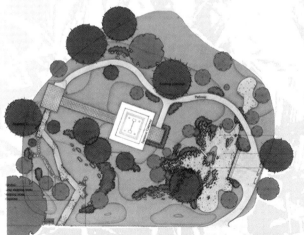

Kew's decorative buildings

When they were built, the decorative buildings at Kew represented all the fervent interest and excitement of knowledge newly gained in a widening world. China and the Islamic world were opening up. There was a revival of classicism through the 'Grand Tour' taken by 18th century gentry. This passion for the newly-discovered influenced the influential in the design and development of the Gardens at Kew. The ornamental features at Kew are an eclectic collection and should be looked at in the context of their period. Past plans and illustrations show that so many have come and gone, that fervent thanks should be given for those that remain.

THE CHAMBERS' COLLECTION

The Ruined Arch, Temple of Bellona and the Temple of Arethusa were all designed and constructed by Sir William Chambers (see p 63). The Temple of Aeolus is a Chambers' design, but was moved and reconstructed on its artificial mound by Decimus Burton in 1845. They are all Grade II listed buildings.

THE RUINED ARCH is a charming folly built in 1759 as a fashionable mock ruin.

THE TEMPLE OF BELLONA (1760) is named after the Roman goddess of war. Behind its Doric facade is a room decorated with plaques bearing the names of British and Hanoverian regiments which distinguished themselves in the Seven Years' War (1756-63).

THE TEMPLE OF ARETHUSA (1758) Arethusa was a nymph, an attendant on Diana the Huntress. When a river god tried to seduce Arethusa as she bathed, she called to Diana for help and was transformed into a fountain.

THE TEMPLE OF AEOLUS (1760-63) Aeolus was the mythical king of storms and winds, inventor of sails and a great astronomer. The temple once had a revolving seat to provide a panoramic view with very little effort.

Ruined Arch

Temple of Bellona

Temple of Arethusa

Temple of Aeolus

THE FLAG POLE

This 68 m (225 ft) flagpole is Britain's tallest. It was presented to Kew by British Columbia, to celebrate the Canadian province's centenary (1958) and Kew's bicentenary (1959). The Douglas fir from Copper Canyon on Vancouver Island was around 370 years old when cut and weighed 37 tonnes. After being towed up the Thames and shaping at Kew, it was a 'mere' 15 tonnes. It was erected by the 23rd Field Squadron of the Royal Engineers on 5th November 1959. The Union Flag is flown on royal birthdays and anniversaries and on state occasions.

KING WILLIAM'S TEMPLE

Built in 1837 by Sir Jeffry Wyatville to complement Chambers' Temple of Victory (no longer standing), this stone building with its Tuscan porticos contains iron plaques commemorating British military victories from Minden to Waterloo.

King William's Temple

THE ICE HOUSE

Records say that the Ice House, in the heart of the Winter Garden, was in use in 1763. A door, of thick wood for insulation, opened up the north-facing entrance tunnel and the whole brick-lined structure was covered with earth. Winter ice was collected from Kew's original lake, and it took three days to store the 'harvest'. The ice - a great luxury - was packed in with straw and lasted long enough to be used in summer to cool drinks and keep food fresh.

THE CAMPANILE

One of the 39 listed buildings at Kew, the Campanile is in the Italianate Romanesque style of stock brick with red brick dressings. This classical 'bell tower' was designed by Decimus Burton as a disguised chimney for the Palm House boilers 100 m away. A tunnel for both the flue and a railway to carry coal linked the two buildings. Today, it carries hot water piped to the Palm House heaters from modern boilers near the Victoria Gate Centre.

DECIMUS BURTON
(1800-1881)

A brilliant architect from an early age, Burton was the son of a London builder. As the supervising architect at Kew, he designed the Palm House in conjunction with Richard Turner (see p 26), the Temperate House, Museum of Economic Botany, and Main Gate, worked with William Nesfield on the design for the Broad Walk (see p 56) and restored the Temple of Aeolus.

Campanile

KEW'S GATES

Four of Kew's gates are Grade II listed - the Main Gate, designed by Decimus Burton in 1845 and completed the next year; the Lion Gate and Lodge, the Unicorn Gate, and the Victoria Gate, the latter three all being built during the second half of the 19th century.

Burton's Main Gate on Kew Green signified a change of attitude on the part of Kew's management, because Sir William Hooker, when he became Director, no longer required visitors to be escorted by gardeners. At the end of his first year, some 9,000 people passed through this grand entrance with its coat of arms and ornamental foliage.

The London and South Western Railway reached Richmond; another branch from Brentford to Willesden brought passengers to 'Kew Junction', river steamers stopped at Kew for the Gardens; and by 1850, annual attendance had reached the heady heights of more than 150,000 visitors.

There is as much history behind Kew's gates as there is in the Gardens. They tell of expansion, of demands for public access and above all, of a fine monumental design tradition that is as impressive today as it was when they were built.

THE QUEEN'S BEASTS

These ten heraldic figures in front of the Palm House are Portland stone replicas of those which stood at Westminster Abbey during the coronation of H.M. Queen Elizabeth II. By the same sculptor, the late James Woodford, they were presented anonymously to the gardens in 1956. The beasts, selected from the armorial bearings of many of the Queen's forbears, are judged to best illustrate her royal lineage. From right to left, seen with the Pond behind the onlooker, they are:-

The Falcon of the Plantagenets

The Black Bull of Clarence

The Griffin of Edward III

The Unicorn of Scotland

The White Lion of Mortimer

The Lion of England

The White Horse of Hanover

The Red Dragon of Wales

The Yale of Beaufort

The White Greyhound of Richmond.

The Palm House Pond

The Palm House Pond was part of the major transformation of Kew in 1845, under William Nesfield and Decimus Burton. Enlarged and reshaped, it provided a water feature in its own right, and a balance to the formal parterres. It also reflected the entire length of the Palm House in its waters, adding to the focal importance of the magnificent building. A simple fountain was added in 1853. The siting of the Pond was a masterstroke, the unity of it and the Palm House now recognised all over the world.

Hercules wrestling the river-god Achelous

69

KEW PALACE

Kew has had royal associations since 1718 , when the Prince and Princess of Wales, (later to become King George II and Queen Caroline), having been banished from St. James's Palace by George I, moved into a splendid riverside house and renamed it Richmond Lodge.

After George I died, Queen Caroline leased several parcels of land and buildings. These included the Dutch House, built around 1631 with distinctive Flemish bond brickwork and rounded gables, by Samuel Fortrey, a merchant of Dutch origin. This building is now known as Kew Palace.

George II and Queen Caroline's son, Prince Frederick, married Princess Augusta and it was she who effectively established the botanic gardens of today. Her son, George III was the first British monarch to separate court and home. In 1781, he bought the Dutch House to accommodate his expanding family. It became the family home, where his wife Charlotte gave birth to George IV.

After Queen Charlotte died in 1818, Kew Palace was closed. In December 1896, Queen Victoria agreed to Kew's acquisition of the Palace, providing there was no alteration to the room in which Queen Charlotte died. In 1898, the palace passed to the Department of Works and opened to the public.

Kew Palace is in the trust of Historic Royal Palaces. The exterior of the palace has been historically restored and is today in fine order, but the interior is being extensively renovated, so is closed to the public at the time of writing. The charming Queen's Garden behind the palace is described in more detail on p 51.

QUEEN CHARLOTTE'S COTTAGE

The origins of this cottage may well been the single storey building provided for the Menagerie keeper - more of the Menageries a little later. There is no doubt that Queen Charlotte was given the building in 1761 when she married George III and that she extended the property upwards by a floor and also in length.

The picturesque house in its 'country vernacular' style was used by the family as a shelter, and for snacks and occasional meals. The large ground floor room had Hogarth prints on the walls, removed in the 1890s but replaced in 1978. A curved staircase leads to the picnic room, with painted flowers climbing the walls and bamboo motif pelmets and door frames.

The cottage remained private until 1898, when Queen Victoria ceded it and its 15 hectares (37 acres) to Kew. The grounds had rarely been visited; trees were lying where they had fallen, and one condition the Queen made was that the grounds should be kept in their naturalistic state.

o cottage

This condition was supported by the Linnaean Society on behalf of all ornithologists to maintain the area as a suburban haven for birds. That is how today's Conservation Area first came into being (see pp 58-61) and how one of London's finest bluebell woods is kept intact.

Queen Charlotte's Cottage is maintained and administered separately from Kew by Historic Royal Palaces and opening times are limited.

ROYAL MENAGERIES AT KEW

Exotic creatures, as well as newly discovered plants, have been prized collectors' items since exploration began. Charles II had an aviary in St James's Park - hence Birdcage Walk - and the Hanoverian kings who followed were no exceptions in their interest in wild things.

Early records from 1730 citing bills for "feeding Tygers in the Royal paddock Garden" confirm that Queen Caroline had a Menagerie at Kew. In 1760, Chambers designed an aviary next to Princess Augusta's Menagerie, an oval enclosure lined with cages for exotic pheasants and bigger birds, with a large pond for goldfish and more delicate waterfowl. George III's 'New Menagerie' in 1770 was a three acre paddock, with an oval ring of bird pens and the small building that became Queen's Cottage. Birds with colourful plumage featured strongly, but also on display were cattle from Algeria and India and "a hog like a porcupine in skin, with navel on back"; but its most prized occupants were the kangaroos. Chambers' Menagerie became a lawn in 1785 and by 1805, the animal collections had been entirely dispersed.

Today, ornamental waterfowl and decorative fish can still be seen in various parts of the Gardens, but Kew is primarily concerned with the conservation of native species.

PLANTS+PEOPLE, THE ORANGERY

When Sir William Hooker became Kew's first Director in 1841, he set about persuading the administrators of the need for a museum of economic botany, demonstrating the importance of plants to mankind.

In 1846, he displayed his own personal collection of specimens of textiles, gums, dyes and timbers in a fruit store and servants' quarters given to Kew by the Royal Family. Decimus Burton was then asked to adapt part of the building into the new Museum of Economic Botany, which opened on 20th September 1847 to instant success.

Collections grew with contributions from the Great Exhibition in 1851 and the Paris Exhibition of 1855. It soon became clear that the Museum was too small and Decimus Burton was asked to design a new Museum, twice the size, opposite the Palm House. Perversely, this new 1857 Museum was called Museum No. 1, with the first renamed as Museum No. 2 - now the School of Horticulture.

ECONOMIC BOTANY

The study of plants used by people has formed an important part of the work of the Royal Botanic Gardens since the time of George III. In the 19th century, its aim was to aid the economic growth of the British Empire.

Today, its focus is on the sustainable use of plants and on conservation. Much work is undertaken on potential sources of medicinal drugs. There is a real need to preserve trees in Africa for firewood in the 21st century, since most staple foods need to be cooked. As fuelwood supplies diminish, more vegetation is cleared resulting in damaged and degraded habitats.

Economic botany is a close study of the plants that people grow and use. The Economic Botany Collections at Kew are the oldest and largest in the world and are of global significance. They consist of over 70,000 plant specimens, products made from plants, and tools used in their cultivation and processing.

PLANTS+PEOPLE EXHIBITION

This fascinating and highly accessible exhibition gives visitors a glimpse into Kew's collections and emphasises their importance. It serves as a timely reminder of the close relationship between plants and people in every aspect of their lives.

MUTINY ON THE BOUNTY

Breadfruit was introduced to the West Indies from its native Tahiti to feed plantation slaves. Sir Joseph Banks - then botanical adviser to Kew - chose Captain Bligh to sail and collect breadfruit seedlings in 1789. The mutiny on his ship, HMS Bounty, delayed the breadfruit's arrival until 1792. What's more, the slaves preferred plantains.

THE ORANGERY

This 1761 building is the earliest at Kew designed by Sir William Chambers and also the largest classical style building in the Gardens, measuring 28 m (92 ft) long by 10 m (33 ft) deep.

Princess Augusta's coat of arms was placed over the central bay of the facade in the 1840s, along with the Royal Arms and escutcheons with the monogram 'A' in honour of Queen Adelaide, wife of William IV.

Designed to hold orange trees, the light levels inside the building were too low to grow plants, even after glass doors were added at either end in 1842. Today, it is a deservedly popular, elegant café-restaurant.

Kew's art galleries

Botanists have always needed artists. Plants die, dried specimens fade, but botanical art records plants in detail for posterity. Some botanical artists are professionals, taken on collecting expeditions; some are gifted amateurs making their own 'collections' of paintings and drawings for their own satisfaction.

THE MARIANNE NORTH GALLERY

Marianne North was a highly talented amateur with a great eye for detail. She learned to enjoy travel with her father, the MP for Hastings, whom she accompanied on his tours of Europe and the Middle East.

She was given lessons in flower painting by a Dutch woman artist and by Valentine Bartholomew, Flower-painter-in-Ordinary to Queen Victoria. On the death of her father, whom she described as "the one idol and friend of my life", she started her travels at the age of 40 and, with several letters of introduction, began her search for the world's exotic flora.

Her travels were relentless, her productivity seemingly inexhaustible. Her first solo trip in 1871 saw her in Jamaica and North America; her next to Brazil; then Japan in 1875, returning home through Sarawak, Java and Ceylon. India inspired her to 200 paintings of buildings as well as plants.

She sketched rapidly in pen and ink on heavy paper, then the oils would come straight from the tube. Her palette was of bold and assertive colours and her enthusiasm evident, and just occasionally rather undisciplined.

She liked to paint plants "in their homes" in ecological settings with the addition of an occasional insect or other small creature; and sometimes against a mountain background.

In August 1879, Marianne North wrote to Sir Joseph Hooker, offering Kew not only her collection of paintings, but also a gallery in which to house them, her only stipulation being the use of a room as a studio. Kew, of course, accepted.

Her architect friend James Fergusson designed a gallery which mirrored her feelings for India, providing a verandah around the outside of the building; while satisfying his own ideas on lighting with large clerestory windows high above the paintings.

Miss North took charge of the hanging herself, arranging them in geographical order over a dado of 246 vertical strips of different timbers. The walls are virtually solid with paintings - there are 832 artworks all told, showing over 900 species of plants - a unique memorial to an equally unique woman.

KEW GARDENS GALLERY

Located in Cambridge Cottage, Kew Gardens Gallery has exhibitions of botanical art by past and contemporary artists, and other subjects, such as the graphically exciting London Transport posters which have regularly featured trips to Kew since 1908.

Because many of the facilities in Cambridge Cottage may be hired for private use, such as weddings and other receptions (see p 90), the Gallery can occasionally be closed to the public.

What's in a name?

THE SYSTEM AT KEW

Plants are known by a variety of names. They have both common names and scientific or Latin names. There's room for confusion as the same plant may be called by different common names. This is obvious with different countries and languages, but the same plant may have many regional names in the same country. For example, here in the UK, bird's-foot trefoil (*Lotus corniculatus*) is also known as hen and chickens, Tom Thumb, granny's toenails, cuckoo's stockings, and Dutchman's clogs. But any botanist, from Aberystwyth to Zagreb, knows what is meant by *Lotus corniculatus.*

Again, an English bluebell, like those in the woods at Kew, is *Hyacinthoides non-scripta*, but in Scotland a bluebell is *Campanula rotundifolia*, a delicate little flower of dry grassy places. In England, however, *Campanula rotundifolia* is a harebell.

The advantage of the scientific name is that it's recognised everywhere. The advantage of a *Latin* scientific name is that as Latin is a dead language, it cannot change its meaning, but, at the same time, is very descriptive. There are no political or nationalistic overtones in Latin, either, so it is readily accepted throughout the world.

THE LINNAEAN BREAKTHROUGH

The Swedish botanist Carolus Linnaeus (1707-78) is credited with the naming system used today for all living organisms - plants and animals. He was the first to group organisms into a logical hierarchy based on shared similarities. His plant classification was based on flower parts and remained unchallenged for about 200 years until the works of Charles Darwin and Gregor Mendel, with their respective theories of evolution and genetic inheritance, led to the desire to produce a *phylogenetic* classification, one which reflects evolutionary changes.

Nowadays, with DNA research undertaken at Kew, plants are also being grouped into their relationships according to differences in their genetic fingerprints (see p 83).

RECOGNISING PLANTS

A typical label showing the system used within the Royal Botanic Gardens, both at Kew and at Wakehurst Place. Here, it refers to the plant shown immediately on the right.

Collector's or donor's code and plant's collection number

Plant family

Accession number: a unique number given to each plant or group of plants in Kew's collection

1992-123 HHME	CAMPANULACEAE
"PEACH-LEAVED BELLFLOWER" Campanula persicifolia	
• N	N. ASIA, EUROPE

Plant's natural distribution range

N shows that the plant originated from wild source material

Common name

•signifies that the identity of the plant has been verified by a botanist at Kew

Scientific name shows genus and then species

76

Campanula persicifolia L.
Lavey le... ...1906.

PREDICTIVE TAXONOMY

The study of plant classification is called 'taxonomy' and it's carried out by taxonomists. Phylogenetic classification, based on relatedness, can be *predictive*. It happened with drugs from plants that may help with AIDS. An important chemical called castanospermine was found in an Australian tree in the genus *Castanospermum*. Taxonomists at Kew predicted that the chemical, or something very similar, might be found in the related Amazonian plant *Alexa* and were proved correct.

CLASSIFY OR DIE

There's a very basic human need to classify things. It probably developed in the hunter-gatherer days, when plants had to be classified into edible and poisonous, and that knowledge needed to be passed on in order to survive. Food, magic, medicine, fire, use as tools or weapons - different plants had different properties.

The ancient Greeks had words for plants. Theophrastus (d. 287 BC) classified, in a very basic way, the 500-odd plants in the Athens botanic garden, while Dioscorides (c. 40-90 AD) wrote the first herbal, *Materia Medica*, which was used for about 1,000 years.

BASICS OF CLASSIFICATION

With plants, the basic group is a *species*, with a unique combination of leaf, stem, flower, fruit and seed characteristics. Species are often found in a particular geographical area and don't usually interbreed. When species have general characteristics in common, they are themselves grouped into a *genus* (plural *genera*). Several genera with basics in common can be put into a larger group, called a *family*, such as 'grasses' or 'bellflowers'.

The Order Beds (see p 49) are the ideal place to learn more about taxonomy because here, members of the same family are planted together so their similarities and differences can be seen very easily.

LEARNING LATIN FROM PLANTS

Plants have first a genus name, like a surname, then a species name, which is like a given name. The two names identify the plant and often describe it entertainingly, the Latin giving excellent clues as to its derivation. For example:-

GIANT HORSETAIL

Equisetum giganteum, coming from *Equus*, horse and *setum*, bristle, together with *giganteum*, giant.

DAISY

Bellis perennis, coming from *bellus*, pretty and *perennis*, perennial.

STINKING IRIS

Iris foetidissima, coming from iris, a rainbow for the many colours of the flower and *foetid*, smelly with *-issima*, most - the smelliest!

The history of Kew

I: THE ESTATES

The very early history of Kew Gardens from 1718 is touched on in the story of Kew Palace (see p70), and taken up here with the marriage of King George II's son, Frederick, Prince of Wales, to Princess Augusta of Saxe-Gotha in 1736, when they lived in the White House, originally next door to what is now Kew Palace.

Frederick and Augusta were garden enthusiasts, and were helped by the Earl of Bute, who advised them on obtaining plants and landscaping and then became the 'finishing tutor' to the Wales's son, later George III.

Princess Augusta

GRAND PLANS

The Wales's garden increased in both content and ambition. With his dilettante interest in art, literature and science, Frederick's 1750 plans for the garden embraced trees, exotics, and a wish for an aqueduct and a "mound to be adorned with the statues or busts of all these philosophers and to represent the Mount of Parnassus."

Before these plans could be realised, he died, after a bout of pleurisy and from a burst abscess in his chest, possibly caused by a blow from a cricket ball some considerable time earlier. His death was lamented by England's gardening fraternity and the botanist Dr John Mitchell declared that "Planting and Botany in England would be the poorer for his Passing."

PRINCESS AUGUSTA AND GEORGE III

In 1752, Princess Augusta instructed her head gardener, John Dillman, to complete the works planned by her late husband. With the very able help of the Earl of Bute, the development of Kew as a serious botanic garden was well under way, driven by Bute's desire to have a garden which would " … contain all the plants known on Earth." Princess Augusta was, in effect, the founder of the botanic gardens at Kew.

Bute introduced the Princess to William Chambers, an ambitious young architect who had previously submitted plans for a projected mausoleum for her dead husband, and in 1757, Chambers was appointed tutor in architecture to the future George III, who came to the throne in 1760. See p63 for more on Chambers and pp66-70 for his decorative buildings.

With his succession, George III inherited the Kew and Richmond estates and appointed his 'Dearest Friend' Lord Bute a Privy Councillor, while Chambers became Controller of the King's Works.

In 1764, Capability Brown, now Master Gardener at Hampton Court, was instructed to redesign Richmond Gardens. In creating his 'natural' landscapes, Brown removed most of the decorative buildings, 18 houses in West Sheen and the whole of the riverside terrace. He was almost universally disliked for this at the time, but 20 years later, the mature gardens were admired, typifying the clash of styles; the formal decorative against the 'new' naturalistic.

William Aiton, Head Gardener
to Princess Augusta

The Botanic Garden became part of the Royal Household in 1801 and Richmond Gardens and Kew Gardens were formally united in 1802. The great benefactor Sir Joseph Banks was exerting his benign influence at Kew and William Aiton was Head Gardener - see following pages.

The next forty years saw the Prince Regent become George IV, to be succeeded by William IV and then, in 1837, Queen Victoria. After a period of decline from 1820, when Banks died, Kew was given to

the nation in 1840, when it was transferred to the Office of Woods and Forests.

With the appointment of Sir William Hooker as its first Director, another era had begun at Kew. The people most responsible for shaping the present Kew Gardens were soon in place; Sir William Hooker, Decimus Burton with Richard Turner, and William Nesfield. Their contributions are amply covered earlier in this book.

THE 20TH CENTURY
The scientific and conservationist pedigree of Kew is wonderfully illustrated by the presentation in 1899, by the Natal Botanic Garden, of an *Encephalartos woodii*, now described as the rarest plant in cultivation at Kew, and possibly the world's last surviving specimen.

In the century's early years, more glasshouses were built for collections, scientific work continued and the Director of Kew was appointed botanical advisor to the Colonial Office, shortly before the Gardens were transferred to the Board of Agriculture and Fisheries.

The Gardens have been interrupted in their growth from time to time. Suffragettes burnt down the Refreshment Pavilion in 1913. There was a violent storm in 1916, a drought in 1921, an exceptionally heavy snowfall in 1926 and the Great Storm of 1987 did considerable damage.

But Kew survives and among the many high spots have been the restorations of the Palm and Temperate Houses, and the building of the Princess of Wales Conservatory and the new Alpine House. The gaining of the management of Wakehurst Place, Sussex, allowed some much-needed expansion for both plants and conservation projects. The less harsh growing conditions let many genera, unsuited to Kew, flourish and it was there that the Millennium Seed Bank was established. There is more on Wakehurst Place on pp 92-93.

THE SWAN BOAT
Made to celebrate the future George III's 17th birthday in 1755, the swan's head was 18 ft (5.4 m) high and the boat large enough to carry ten people on the Lake.

2: The Collections

The harmony of Kew today is thanks to a succession of avid collectors, visionary curators, inspired landscape architects and redoubtable gardeners using their talents as the gardens have grown and developed over the centuries.

The direction of Kew changed from the simple collecting and showing of exotics, to the serious scientific and economic botanical purposes of Sir Joseph Banks and the two Hookers who saw Kew as a centre for developing the natural resources of the Empire. Kew gardeners found themselves on opposite sides in the mutiny on the Bounty (see p73). Kew collectors went to South America to collect cinchona and rubber for transfer to India.

Sir Joseph Banks (1743-1820)
A wealthy entrepreneur and natural history enthusiast, Banks went on several collecting expeditions including, between 1768-71, James Cook's round the world expedition in the *Endeavour*. He paid for his own passage and those of eight companions, including botanists, artists and a secretary.

He was elected President of the Royal Society in 1778 and held the post for 41 years. He used his influence, taking on, in his words, "a kind of superintendence" to promote the Gardens at Kew and without his guidance, it is doubtful if Kew would have evolved into the internationally respected institution it is today.

Systematic collecting
Faced with competition from other European botanic gardens, Banks resolved that new plants should always be seen first at Kew and so organised systematic collecting expeditions throughout the world. He also asked diplomats, army and navy officers, merchants and missionaries to remember Kew on their travels.

Under Banks' directions, Francis Masson went to South Africa and North America;

Robert Brown and Peter Good journeyed to Australia and William Kerr started collecting in China. Two more, Allen Cunningham and James Bowie, spent two highly productive years in Brazil collecting bromeliads and orchids.

Banks' last visit to Kew
In 1819, Banks visited Kew for the last time, specifically to see a plant that Franci Masson had introduced in 1775; the African cycad *Encephalartos altensteinii* which had just produced its very first cone, 44 years after arriving. Sir Joseph Banks died on 19 June 1820.

Wardian cases
Sealed glass cases named after their inventor, Nathaniel Ward, were absolutely key to the transfer of living plants from the furthest corners of the world back to Kew. They were used first in 1835 and last in 1962 to bring plants from Fiji.

When Sir William Hooker took charge of Kew in 1840 after a period of neglect, collecting started again in earnest. With Burton's new buildings, ailing plants were revived and room was made for more.

Joseph Hooker, Sir William's son, was an avid explorer and collector who later took over as Director from his father. In 1853, some 4,500 herbaceous plants were in cultivation. By 1864, there were 13,000 and more species, with over 3,000 species of trees and shrubs in the Arboretum.

NEW ADDITIONS

Since Sir William Hooker, Kew's emphasis has been on collecting for the purposes of economic botany. Today's living collections at Kew are scientific resources used for research by botanists in the Herbarium and the Jodrell Laboratory (see pp 82-85). The palm collection is particularly fine as a result of botanical expeditions and similar expeditions are still sent out from Kew to bring back specimens collected under guidelines laid down by the Convention on Biological Diversity.

FAMOUS FLOWERINGS

The giant arum, *Amorphophallus titanum*, shown right, flowered in June 1889, for the first time ever outside its native Sumatra. Subsequent flowerings, in June 1901, July 1926 and 1996 attracted crowds, but visitors never stay long, due to its truly disgusting odour.

In 1991, *Agave americana* flowered in the Princess of Wales Conservatory, where panes of glass had to be removed to allow the flower stem to keep growing.

A coconut fruited in the Palm House for the first time in 1993 and the following year, *Ensete superbum* also flowered for the first time.

In spring, the luminous green flower tresses of one of Kew's rarest plants, the jade vine (*Strongylodon macrobotrys*), shown left, dangle from the Palm House roof. Scientists from Kew's Jodrell Laboratory have pollinated the flowers to develop seeds, but the identity of its natural pollinator in the rainforests of the Philippines is still a mystery.

The role of Kew today

RESEARCH, CONSERVATION AND EDUCATION

The work carried out at Kew from the 1980s onwards, when responsibility was given to a Board of Trustees (1984), has been building up to that being undertaken today, at the start of a new century, when conservation in all its forms has assumed the greatest importance.

The vital role that plants play in the ecosystem is not lost on world leaders. The Convention on Biological Diversity, which Britain ratified in 1994, requires signatories actively to promote understanding and awareness of biological diversity and the need for conservation.

Kew plays a significant role in this 'active promotion' and nowhere are Kew's aims more clearly laid down than in the Mission Statement.

Behind the text on these pages runs a simple maxim; *"All life depends on plants."*

KEW'S MISSION
To enable better management of the Earth's environment by increasing knowledge and understanding of the plant and fungal kingdoms - the basis of life on earth.

This will be achieved by:

- developing our global reference collections and making them more accessible to the greatest possible variety and number of users;

- undertaking world-wide research into systematics, economic and ethnobotany, biological interactions, conservation and horticulture;

- supporting the conservation and sustainable use of plant resources in the UK and overseas;

- informing the wider public about our activities, through the maintenance and development of world-class Gardens that provide a window into our work;

- providing education, advice and information in various forms to our stakeholders, and building the global capacity for studying and conserving plant diversity through collaborative partnerships and by training scientists from developing countries.

WHY RESEARCH?

By studying plant structures, genetic material and biochemistry, relationships between plants can be clarified, leading to many practical applications. At Kew, plant anatomy, cytogenetics and other laboratory-based research is carried out in the Jodrell Laboratory. Located between the Alpine House and the Order Beds, it is not open to the public, but it is possible to see the laboratory in action from the colonnade.

In the Herbarium, plants are identified, named and classified, resulting in detailed studies of particular groups of plants - how they interrelate, and how they differ from each other. Carrying out surveys of vegetation in many different parts of the world is the very foundation of other plant research or conservation projects. The Herbarium, not open to the public, attracts an average of 50 researchers from around the world every week.

GENETIC 'FINGERPRINTING'

Kew is at the cutting edge of research. Scientists in the Jodrell Laboratory have pioneered techniques using the chemicals that plants naturally produce to reveal relationships between them.

Another technique involves treating plant tissues by 'painting' their chromosomes with special dyes which glow under a microscope's light. Different colours identify the unique chromosomes from different plants and the parents of a hybrid can be traced this way. Genetic fingerprinting makes use of the built-in instructions each plant has for making chlorophyll. Each plant species has its own set of instructions and when different sets are compared, close matches reveal close relationships. Results often confirm current thinking, but occasionally previously unknown relationships have been revealed.

A VITAL ROLE, BEAUTIFULLY PACKAGED

Through research, Kew's scientists are constantly taking enormously important steps towards harnessing the abilities of plants not only to feed the world more effectively, but to help fight disease and other problems.

Kew's role, then, is predominantly in gaining and distributing knowledge of the plant kingdom and its relationship to mankind. That this globally vital role is so beautifully and interestingly packaged at Kew and at Wakehurst Place, is a bonus for all of us.

Working in partnership to conserve seeds

Kew today

In the past, most botanic gardens promoted economic botany. Others, Kew prominent among them, also established herbaria and supported taxonomists on their expeditions to collect, identify and classify the world's plants. This mammoth task has continued over the centuries and today, as the world faces a growing environmental crisis, the work of botanic gardens becomes more deeply involved in conservation and the sustainable use of ecosystems.

PLANT COLLECTIONS

Living collections of plants have become a vital part of botanical research and conservation. At Kew, the collection of 31,000 taxa, or groups of plants, contains 15 species that are totally extinct in the wild, and 2,000 more included in lists of threatened and endangered species. Kew's work on micropropagation - multiplying plants by reproducing them from buds or tiny seeds - leading to eventual reintroduction in the wild, is critically important to biodiversity.

Kew holds more than living plants, as can be realised from the great numbers of carefully preserved specimens, both old and recently collected, in the Herbarium. There are currently some 7 million specimens in the Herbarium, representing 98% of all the known *genera* (groups of similar species) in the world. The mycological specimen collection of 800,000 mushrooms, toadstools and other fungi, is one of the largest and most important in the world.

ECONOMIC BOTANY

Kew's Economic Botany Collection was started by Sir William Hooker, Kew's first Director, over 150 years ago (see pp 72-73). The 76,000 items include one of the finest wood collections in the world (32,000 samples from 12,000 species), thousands of bottles of oils, and thousands of other plant-based artifacts and oddities. It is housed in the Joseph Banks Building, named after Kew's great benefactor (see pp 80-81), and is a high-tech earth-covered complex on a three acre site. It is not open to the public, but many items from the collection are on view in the Plants+People Exhibition in Museum No 1.

CONSERVATION AND SUSTAINABLE USE

Kew also houses a wealth of information about plant distribution and usage and scientists here are building up a database on useful plants for arid regions. This provides vital help in Kew's work towards, for instance, sustainable crop production through the Plantas Nordeste project in semi-arid country in north-eastern Brazil.

Kew is also identifying plants to cultivate for fuelwood in Zimbabwe and rattans for more effective use in cane furniture in south-east Asia. Plants are investigated as sources of useful chemicals, for medicines or to repel plant-eating insects.

Kew's Seed Bank, recently transferred to the Millennium Seed Bank at Wakehurst Place (see p 93) is yet another example of crucially important conservation work.

Conservation and sustainable use are the watchwords behind Kew's work today. Kew acts as adviser to the UK government on the Convention on International Trade in Endangered Species of Flora and Fauna (CITES) and also on international conservation legislation. Conservation genetics is important work at Kew, looking at the genetic diversity of populations of endangered plants, to avoid interbreeding and so make sure the populations remain as healthy as possible.

Kew's work, then, as in its early days, still embraces classification of the world's plants and the promotion of economic botany. Today, though, the emphasis is not on economic botany for the growth of 'Empire', but more for the benefit of mankind as a whole.

THE HERBARIUM

Originally named Hunter House, this 18th Century building became the home of the Herbarium and Library in 1853. To house ever-expanding collections, wings were added in 1877, 1903 and 1968, with further expansion into the quadrangle in 1989.

EXTINCT BRITISH GRASS GROWS AT KEW

Extinct in the wild, having been seen last in 1963, *Bromus interruptus* is, for botanists, the UK's most famous grass. It is being grown in Kew's living collections and is a subject of an English Nature's Species Recovery Programme, managed by Kew.

Vast numbers of plants have been preserved in the Herbarium on Herbarium Sheets. A well-collected herbarium specimen comprises the vital parts of the plant - flowers and fruits - as well as some leaves attached to the stem. The label - essential to the collection - carries field notes, the collector's name, a serial number and other important details. The Herbarium Sheet for *Bromus interruptus* is shown here.

Kew today

It is one of Kew's stated aims to increase people's understanding of the plant kingdom and so education is seen as playing an absolutely key role. So much so, that 'education' at Kew is divided into three: Higher Education and Training; Public Education and Interpretation; and Schools Education, in order to meet the needs of different audiences.

People come to Kew for a variety of reasons. Casual visitors are different from garden enthusiasts wanting to learn more; these are different from professionals from all over the world seeking further high level training; and different again from university students visiting to find out more about Kew's research activities.

PUTTING PLANTS ON THE CURRICULUM

What Kew realises is that if environmental and conservation issues are to be kept alive in this new century, it is vital to inform and influence today's schoolchildren. It is they - tomorrow's consumers, teachers, business people, opinion-formers and politicians - who will be shaping the future of the planet.

More than 60,000 schoolchildren visit Kew and Wakehurst in booked groups each year, armed with work sheets and education packs, or enjoying even greater

At Kew's School of Horticulture, students can gain the three-year Kew Diploma of Horticulture, and prestigious research degrees can be gained here, too. There is an expanding programme of 'Capacity Building', whereby international students are provided with essential training and practical experience in, for example, herbarium techniques and botanic garden management.

rewards from a tour guided by one of Kew's teaching team. Museum No 1, where the Plants+People Exhibition regularly astounds visitors of all ages, let alone schoolchildren, has a popular classroom facility.

At Wakehurst Place, the SEEBOARD Study Centre is designed specially for school groups. Lying deep in the heart of the Sussex countryside, it is surrounded by woods, meadows and wetlands, ideal for ecological studies.

The Outreach Education Programme sees Kew visiting schools, running anything from week-long specially tailored work-shops in a mobile classroom, to a single talk loaded with specimens and demonstrations and long remembered through the posters and leaflets left behind.

Botany and conservation are very much on today's curriculum. Kew's mission in education is to make the plant kingdom interesting, fun - and important. Caught young, children are conservationists for life

THE SCIENCE BEHIND THE SHOWPIECE

Kew's Director, Professor Peter Crane, plans to extend the role of education throughout the Gardens, but not in any didactic sense.

"I want people to be involved with Kew. Visiting should be a beautiful, aesthetic experience with world-class horti-culture. But we should also intrigue people with the plant kingdom and show them that it is extremely vulnerable. We must put across the message how important plants are, and the crucial relationship between people and plants. We have a wonderful library, but need a public reading room. We will allow people behind the scenes to see the work going on because the scientific work and public education should be mutually supportive. We have a huge living collection of plants from all over the world and I would like to make them relevant to everyone."

How Kew is funded

KEW'S WORK BENEFITS THE WHOLE WORLD, AND YOU CAN BE PART OF IT.

"Today the Royal Botanic Gardens, Kew, is increasingly involved in the conservation of our environment as thousands of species of plants face extinction. And the simple fact is that without plants, human life on this earth will cease to exist.

Kew's botanists and horticulturists are able to solve global problems by advising on environmental management, conserving endangered species, and searching for alternative crops as sources of food, animal fodder, fuel and medicine.

In supporting the Friends, you will be helping to finance the vital work Kew is doing to help save plant life and the world.

Thank you for your support."

Davin Attenborough

The Royal Botanic Gardens, Kew, is a registered charity, set up in April 1984 under the terms of the National Heritage Act, 1983. Responsibility for the Gardens then passed from the Ministry of Agriculture, Fisheries and Food (MAFF) to a Board of Trustees.

This type of arrangement had been proposed twice before, once in 1838, when the Office of Woods and Forests recommended that Kew should be managed by trustees who represented London's educational, scientific and horticultural communities; and again in 1959, when the Ashby Visiting Group favoured an independent grant-aided institution with trustees.

Kew's functions are broadly defined in an Act of Parliament and are today firmly established in the Mission Statement (see p 82). The Gardens continue to be funded in part by MAFF, but faced with diminishing financial support in the late 1980s, the overriding concern at Kew was the securing of adequate funds to maintain the Gardens and its research programmes.

KEW FOUNDATION
In March 1990, Kew Foundation was set up with the sole aim of raising funds for projects not covered by grant aid and self-generated money. The Foundation has proved an unqualified success, raising in excess of £2 million a year towards Kew projects, such as those described on previous pages.

FRIENDS OF KEW

June the same year saw the launch of Friends of Kew, with membership bringing special privileges and opportunities to those wishing to know more about Kew specifically and horticulture generally. Members can also accompany Kew botanists through the plant world on a programme of botanical tours; and extend their interest still further with special events and lectures. Membership income and that generated by fees for various events all contribute much-needed revenue. Over £3.5 millions have been contributed to Kew through membership, gifts and legacies, revenue which has supported projects like the Millennium Seed Bank, protecting threatened species and numbers of features at both Kew and Wakehurst Place. There's no better way of supporting Kew's mission than to become a Friend.

FRIENDS OF KEW –
THE BENEFITS OF BELONGING

For an annual membership fee, Friends of Kew benefit from the following advantages:-

- Unlimited entry to Kew, Wakehurst Place and fourteen other gardens nationwide.

- KEW magazine four times a year, full of lively articles on horticulture, botany and environmental issues and other interesting subjects.

- Free passes to bring guests into the Gardens.

- Discounts in Kew shops, for special events, tours and lectures, plus opportunities to see behind the scenes at Kew.

Details on how to join Friends of Kew are in the leaflets available at the Victoria Gate Centre, the Orangery and on the entry maps handed to visitors. Or call 020 8332 5922.

KEW ENTERPRISES LTD

This is the commercial arm of the Gardens, with the sole purpose of generating funds by profitable trading through the Shops at Kew Gardens and Wakehurst Place, from licensing and events such as the Summer Swing music festival. Kew Enterprises also manages the hiring out of Cambridge Cottage for private functions such as weddings, receptions and business meetings; and of the Temperate House for private and corporate events (see pp 90-91).

Profits made from admission fees taken at the gates, catering, events and purchases from the Shops all help support the scientific work undertaken at Kew.

Kew Explorer

More goes on at Kew than meets the eye. Visitors may wonder why the Kew Gardens Gallery in Cambridge Cottage is closed, but full of people. Late one evening, top deck bus passengers may be intrigued to see the Temperate House ablaze with light. Music may echo through the grounds on balmy summer evenings. Keen gardeners coming to see the plants may be stunned by an outdoor exhibition of exotic sculpture.

The answer to these puzzles is a simple one - special events. Kew Gardens' Special Events Office, working in cooperation with sponsors and other promoters, arranges eagerly awaited events such as 'Summer Swing', deservedly popular picnic evenings in the grounds, listening to bands.

There are four major festivals annually, and past and planned activities include the Orchid Festival, Autumn Harvest, Christmas events and international themes from Africa, Japan and India. They involve storytelling and craftworks, as well as great botanical interest and are among the favourite high spots of Kew's year.

RELATIONSHIPS IN BLOOM - WEDDINGS AT KEW

It's the bride's day, they say, and to judge from their expressions of total delight, the words 'Kew Gardens' and 'fairytale wedding' seem to go together. Cambridge Cottage is licensed to host civil wedding ceremonies and receptions. It can be just the wedding ceremony; the ceremony and reception; or just the reception - the choic is down to the couple and their families.

Kew's helpful staff make the day special. A choice from approved caterers makes sure the reception runs smoothly; while there is no better backdrop for wedding photographs than the wonderful buildings

private functions

nd vistas at Kew. A string quartet on the
awn rounds off a summer wedding
erfectly, and at other times of the year,
here is a choice of function rooms in an
legant, yet welcoming environment that is
teeped in history. For details of weddings
t Kew, call the Special Events Office on
20 8332 5641.

MAKING BUSINESS A PLEASURE
or 'away-from-it-all' strategy meetings or
rainstorming; for important client or
nternal presentations; and for prestige
orporate entertaining, Kew has a growing
eputation. All puns aside, there is
omething dramatic and inspiring about an
legant supper under tall palms in the
emperate House; dark outside, but with
eautiful plants all around theatrically lit to
reate a truly memorable experience.

ambridge Cottage's two rooms can be
rranged in a variety of seating plans and
quipped with projection and audio-visual
quipment as required. Quality catering,
fficient service, excellent facilities and
bove all, a magnificent setting - it really is
pleasure doing business at Kew Gardens.

The Royal Botanic Gardens leased Wakehurst Place from the National Trust in 1965. Set in the beautiful High Sussex Weald, the well-proportioned sandstone manor house with its Elizabethan facade is surrounded by a mixture of formal gardens and woodland walks.

Gerald Loder, the first Lord Wakehurst, was a passionate plantsman who built up an outstanding collection of temperate flora from eastern Asia, South America, Australia and New Zealand between 1903 and 1936. On Loder's death, Wakehurst Place was bought by Sir Henry Price, and in his care, the estate matured richly. Sir Henry left Wakehurst Place, with a sizeable endowment, to the nation in 1963.

Wakehurst Place has a mild, friendly climate, a high rainfall and moisture-retentive soils, allowing many important groups of plants, difficult to grow successfully at Kew, to flourish.

In retrospect, the Great Storm of 1987, in which many of Wakehurst's trees suffered, had a silver lining. It allowed a considered reorganisation of parts of the woodlands, where plantings are now arranged in geographical areas, allowing visitors to walk through realistic forest environments, such as New England's 'fall colour' or the majestic giant redwoods of the Rocky Mountains.

With extensive water gardens, a steep Himalayan Glade, charming walled gardens nearer the mansion and excellent facilities for visitors, Wakehurst Place is a deservedly popular attraction.

But, with Kew's mission for conservation and serious botanical research, it is only to be expected that there is more to Wakehurst Place. And there is.

LODER VALLEY NATURE RESERVE
Already rich in native wildlife, a large part of Wakehurst Place has been designated a Site of Special Scientific Interest by English Nature. The Loder Valley Nature Reserve encompasses three major types of habitat; woodland, meadowland and wetland. Wildlife conservation follows naturally, since each habitat is suited to a different range of birds, mammals and invertebrates.

As a protected area, visits can be made only by prior arrangement, but sightings of badgers, great crested grebes or kingfishers can be virtually guaranteed, depending, of course, on the timing of the visit. This is living conservation and restoration at its best, preserving not only a habitat complete with wildlife, but also traditional countryside management and its resultant crafts and products. Coppicing, for example, not only produces wood for Bar-B-Kew charcoal and country products such as hurdles, besoms and rustic furniture, but has also created a habitat that allows the reintroduction of the native dormouse.

A dormouse at Wakehurst Place - part of English Nature's Species Recovery Programme

Millennium Seed Bank

THE MILLENNIUM SEED BANK

This magnificent £80 million project was part funded by the Millennium Commission and supported by the Wellcome Trust, one of the world's premier medical charities, and Orange plc, together with many other organisations and individuals. Its aim is to conserve biodiversity by storing the seeds of not only every native plant in Britain, but even more importantly, those of some 24,000 other species from around the globe. It is probably the most ambitious conservation project in the world and its interactive exhibition is a magnet for anyone wishing to learn more about plants and their intimate relationship to mankind.

Seeds have an astonishing ability to cling on to life against incredible odds. They'll certainly survive the exceptionally cold and dry conditions in the Millennium Seed Bank vault. Visitors will learn:-

- Why Kew started this international project and its importance to future generations
- How seeds are collected in the wild
- How the laboratories and seed preparation areas go about their work
- How the vaults will safeguard 24,000 plant species for hundreds of years.

The Royal Botanic Gardens, Kew would also like to thank both the National Trust and MAFF, without whose support, this idea would not have turned into the splendid and vitally important reality it has become.

The Wellcome Trust Millennium Building, named after the Wellcome Trust, who have donated over £9 million in recognition of the importance of plants as sources of medical benefits.

LOCATION

Open from 10 a.m. every day of the year except Christmas Day and New Year's Day, Wakehurst Place is around 15 minutes from Junction 10 on the M23, from where it is clearly signposted to just north of Ardingly on the B2028. Haywards Heath station is 6 miles away by taxi and the estate is passed every day of the week by a regular bus service - for current details call Metrobus on 01293 449191.

For the latest information about visiting Wakehurst Place including opening times and admission prices, please visit the website at www.kew.org, email wakehurst@kew.org or telephone 01444 894066 (24 hours).

For more information

NOTES:

Factual details have been checked by an Editorial Committee at the Royal Botanic Gardens, Kew. Kew Gardens and Wakehurst Place are under constant development, so while the general information in this book is accurate at time of going to press, it will be most up to date from the website and telephone numbers given earlier and below.

For ease of reading, the scientific names of plants have generally been omitted from the main body of the text, in favour of common names where they exist.

SOURCES:

The main sources for this souvenir guide have been the leaflets and other communications issued by the Royal Botanic Gardens, Kew; together with the pages and links of Kew's website at www.kew.org

Historical detail and perspective are from Ray Desmond's book 'The History of the Royal Botanic Gardens, Kew'.

Background information, not directly quoted, has come from a variety of sources.

CONTACTING KEW:

Tel: 020 8332 5655

Fax: 020 8332 5610

email: info@kew.org

Web: www.kew.org

'A Sower' by Sir Hamo Thorneycroft

FURTHER READING:

Listed below are books which lead on from many topics in this souvenir guide, to enable anyone interested to follow up and learn more.

'The History of the Royal Botanic Gardens, Kew', by Ray Desmond ISBN 1-86046-529-3, Harvill Press, 1998.

'Sir Joseph Dalton Hooker: Traveller and Plant Collector', by Ray Desmond ISBN 1-85149-305-0, Antique Collectors' Club and RBG Kew, 1999.

'Royal Botanic Gardens, Kew: Gardens for Science and Pleasure', ed. F N Hepper, ISBN 0-11-241181-9, HMSO, 1982.

'In for a penny: a prospect of Kew Gardens, their flora, fauna and falballas', by W Blunt, ISBN 0-241-89823-4, Hamish Hamilton, 1978.

'A Vision of Eden, the Life & Work of Marianne North', ISBN 0-11-250088-9, RBG Kew and HMSO, 1993.

'Marianne North at Kew Gardens, Kew', by Laura Ponsonby, ISBN 0-11-250096-X, RBG Kew and HMSO, 1996.

'The Private Life of Plants' by Sir David Attenborough, ISBN 0-563-37023-8, BBC Books, 1994.

'The Greatest Glasshouse' by Sue Minter, ISBN 0-11-250035-8, HMSO, 1990.

'Plants for People' by Anna Lewington, ISBN 0-565-01094-8, Natural History Museum, 1990.

'Out in the Fields' by A G Atkinson

CREDITS

ISBN 1-84246-020-X

CONCEPT
Paul Cloutman and Michael O'Callaghan.

TEXT
Paul Cloutman.

EDITORIAL PANEL, ROYAL BOTANIC GARDENS, KEW
Dr Pat Griggs, Quincy Leon and James Morley.

DESIGN
Michael O'Callaghan at CDA Design, Worthing.

ILLUSTRATIONS
Except where mentioned, all photographs, graphics and other illustrations are from
libraries and sources owned by the Royal Botanic Gardens, Kew.

Main photography from Kew by Andrew McRobb.

Wildlife photography by Dr Peter Gasson.

Additional photography by James Morley, Paul Cloutman and Michael O'Callaghan:
also, p35 Barry Johnston; weddings, p90 John Paul Holton, p91 Paul Fairbairn-Tennant.

Maps by CDA Design, map features by Paul Collicutt.

Cover illustration, *Paphiopedilum bellatulum* by Pandora Sellars.

Illustrations on pages 7, 8, 11, 12 and 17 by Margaret Stones.

PRINTING
The Bath Press

Typeset in Centaur.

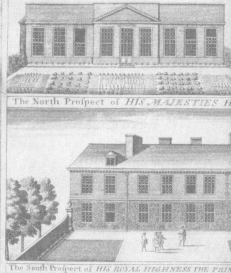